C-146   CAREER EXAMINATION SERIES

This is your
PASSBOOK for...

Clerk-Stenographer

Test Preparation Study Guide
Questions & Answers

COPYRIGHT NOTICE

This book is SOLELY intended for, is sold ONLY to, and its use is RESTRICTED to individual, bona fide applicants or candidates who qualify by virtue of having seriously filed applications for appropriate license, certificate, professional and/or promotional advancement, higher school matriculation, scholarship, or other legitimate requirements of education and/or governmental authorities.

This book is NOT intended for use, class instruction, tutoring, training, duplication, copying, reprinting, excerption, or adaptation, etc., by:

1) Other publishers
2) Proprietors and/or Instructors of "Coaching" and/or Preparatory Courses
3) Personnel and/or Training Divisions of commercial, industrial, and governmental organizations
4) Schools, colleges, or universities and/or their departments and staffs, including teachers and other personnel
5) Testing Agencies or Bureaus
6) Study groups which seek by the purchase of a single volume to copy and/or duplicate and/or adapt this material for use by the group as a whole without having purchased individual volumes for each of the members of the group
7) Et al.

Such persons would be in violation of appropriate Federal and State statutes.

PROVISION OF LICENSING AGREEMENTS – Recognized educational, commercial, industrial, and governmental institutions and organizations, and others legitimately engaged in educational pursuits, including training, testing, and measurement activities, may address request for a licensing agreement to the copyright owners, who will determine whether, and under what conditions, including fees and charges, the materials in this book may be used them. In other words, a licensing facility exists for the legitimate use of the material in this book on other than an individual basis. However, it is asseverated and affirmed here that the material in this book CANNOT be used without the receipt of the express permission of such a licensing agreement from the Publishers. Inquiries re licensing should be addressed to the company, attention rights and permissions department.

All rights reserved, including the right of reproduction in whole or in part, in any form or by any means, electronic or mechanical, including photocopying, recording, or by any information storage and retrieval system, without permission in writing from the Publisher.

Copyright © 2025 by
National Learning Corporation

212 Michael Drive, Syosset, NY 11791
(516) 921-8888 • www.passbooks.com
E-mail: info@passbooks.com

PASSBOOK® SERIES

THE *PASSBOOK® SERIES* has been created to prepare applicants and candidates for the ultimate academic battlefield – the examination room.

At some time in our lives, each and every one of us may be required to take an examination – for validation, matriculation, admission, qualification, registration, certification, or licensure.

Based on the assumption that every applicant or candidate has met the basic formal educational standards, has taken the required number of courses, and read the necessary texts, the *PASSBOOK® SERIES* furnishes the one special preparation which may assure passing with confidence, instead of failing with insecurity. Examination questions – together with answers – are furnished as the basic vehicle for study so that the mysteries of the examination and its compounding difficulties may be eliminated or diminished by a sure method.

This book is meant to help you pass your examination provided that you qualify and are serious in your objective.

The entire field is reviewed through the huge store of content information which is succinctly presented through a provocative and challenging approach – the question-and-answer method.

A climate of success is established by furnishing the correct answers at the end of each test.

You soon learn to recognize types of questions, forms of questions, and patterns of questioning. You may even begin to anticipate expected outcomes.

You perceive that many questions are repeated or adapted so that you can gain acute insights, which may enable you to score many sure points.

You learn how to confront new questions, or types of questions, and to attack them confidently and work out the correct answers.

You note objectives and emphases, and recognize pitfalls and dangers, so that you may make positive educational adjustments.

Moreover, you are kept fully informed in relation to new concepts, methods, practices, and directions in the field.

You discover that you are actually taking the examination all the time: you are preparing for the examination by "taking" an examination, not by reading extraneous and/or supererogatory textbooks.

In short, this PASSBOOK®, used directedly, should be an important factor in helping you to pass your test.

CLERK-STENOGRAPHER

DUTIES
Performs routine stenographic typing and clerical work. Performs related duties as required.

SUBJECT OF EXAMINATION
Written test will cover knowledge, skills, and/or abilities in such areas as:
1. Spelling;
2. Vocabulary
3. English grammar, usage, punctuation
4. Understanding and interpreting written material; and
5. Arithmetic computations.

HOW TO TAKE A TEST

I. YOU MUST PASS AN EXAMINATION

A. *WHAT EVERY CANDIDATE SHOULD KNOW*

Examination applicants often ask us for help in preparing for the written test. What can I study in advance? What kinds of questions will be asked? How will the test be given? How will the papers be graded?

As an applicant for a civil service examination, you may be wondering about some of these things. Our purpose here is to suggest effective methods of advance study and to describe civil service examinations.

Your chances for success on this examination can be increased if you know how to prepare. Those "pre-examination jitters" can be reduced if you know what to expect. You can even experience an adventure in good citizenship if you know why civil service exams are given.

B. *WHY ARE CIVIL SERVICE EXAMINATIONS GIVEN?*

Civil service examinations are important to you in two ways. As a citizen, you want public jobs filled by employees who know how to do their work. As a job seeker, you want a fair chance to compete for that job on an equal footing with other candidates. The best-known means of accomplishing this two-fold goal is the competitive examination.

Exams are widely publicized throughout the nation. They may be administered for jobs in federal, state, city, municipal, town or village governments or agencies.

Any citizen may apply, with some limitations, such as the age or residence of applicants. Your experience and education may be reviewed to see whether you meet the requirements for the particular examination. When these requirements exist, they are reasonable and applied consistently to all applicants. Thus, a competitive examination may cause you some uneasiness now, but it is your privilege and safeguard.

C. *HOW ARE CIVIL SERVICE EXAMS DEVELOPED?*

Examinations are carefully written by trained technicians who are specialists in the field known as "psychological measurement," in consultation with recognized authorities in the field of work that the test will cover. These experts recommend the subject matter areas or skills to be tested; only those knowledges or skills important to your success on the job are included. The most reliable books and source materials available are used as references. Together, the experts and technicians judge the difficulty level of the questions.

Test technicians know how to phrase questions so that the problem is clearly stated. Their ethics do not permit "trick" or "catch" questions. Questions may have been tried out on sample groups, or subjected to statistical analysis, to determine their usefulness.

Written tests are often used in combination with performance tests, ratings of training and experience, and oral interviews. All of these measures combine to form the best-known means of finding the right person for the right job.

II. HOW TO PASS THE WRITTEN TEST

A. NATURE OF THE EXAMINATION

To prepare intelligently for civil service examinations, you should know how they differ from school examinations you have taken. In school you were assigned certain definite pages to read or subjects to cover. The examination questions were quite detailed and usually emphasized memory. Civil service exams, on the other hand, try to discover your present ability to perform the duties of a position, plus your potentiality to learn these duties. In other words, a civil service exam attempts to predict how successful you will be. Questions cover such a broad area that they cannot be as minute and detailed as school exam questions.

In the public service similar kinds of work, or positions, are grouped together in one "class." This process is known as *position-classification*. All the positions in a class are paid according to the salary range for that class. One class title covers all of these positions, and they are all tested by the same examination.

B. FOUR BASIC STEPS

1) Study the announcement

How, then, can you know what subjects to study? Our best answer is: "Learn as much as possible about the class of positions for which you've applied." The exam will test the knowledge, skills and abilities needed to do the work.

Your most valuable source of information about the position you want is the official exam announcement. This announcement lists the training and experience qualifications. Check these standards and apply only if you come reasonably close to meeting them.

The brief description of the position in the examination announcement offers some clues to the subjects which will be tested. Think about the job itself. Review the duties in your mind. Can you perform them, or are there some in which you are rusty? Fill in the blank spots in your preparation.

Many jurisdictions preview the written test in the exam announcement by including a section called "Knowledge and Abilities Required," "Scope of the Examination," or some similar heading. Here you will find out specifically what fields will be tested.

2) Review your own background

Once you learn in general what the position is all about, and what you need to know to do the work, ask yourself which subjects you already know fairly well and which need improvement. You may wonder whether to concentrate on improving your strong areas or on building some background in your fields of weakness. When the announcement has specified "some knowledge" or "considerable knowledge," or has used adjectives like "beginning principles of…" or "advanced … methods," you can get a clue as to the number and difficulty of questions to be asked in any given field. More questions, and hence broader coverage, would be included for those subjects which are more important in the work. Now weigh your strengths and weaknesses against the job requirements and prepare accordingly.

3) Determine the level of the position

Another way to tell how intensively you should prepare is to understand the level of the job for which you are applying. Is it the entering level? In other words, is this the position in which beginners in a field of work are hired? Or is it an intermediate or advanced level? Sometimes this is indicated by such words as "Junior" or "Senior" in the class title. Other jurisdictions use Roman numerals to designate the level – Clerk I, Clerk II, for example. The word "Supervisor" sometimes appears in the title. If the level is not indicated by the title, check the description of duties. Will you be working under very close supervision, or will you have responsibility for independent decisions in this work?

4) Choose appropriate study materials

Now that you know the subjects to be examined and the relative amount of each subject to be covered, you can choose suitable study materials. For beginning level jobs, or even advanced ones, if you have a pronounced weakness in some aspect of your training, read a modern, standard textbook in that field. Be sure it is up to date and has general coverage. Such books are normally available at your library, and the librarian will be glad to help you locate one. For entry-level positions, questions of appropriate difficulty are chosen – neither highly advanced questions, nor those too simple. Such questions require careful thought but not advanced training.

If the position for which you are applying is technical or advanced, you will read more advanced, specialized material. If you are already familiar with the basic principles of your field, elementary textbooks would waste your time. Concentrate on advanced textbooks and technical periodicals. Think through the concepts and review difficult problems in your field.

These are all general sources. You can get more ideas on your own initiative, following these leads. For example, training manuals and publications of the government agency which employs workers in your field can be useful, particularly for technical and professional positions. A letter or visit to the government department involved may result in more specific study suggestions, and certainly will provide you with a more definite idea of the exact nature of the position you are seeking.

III. KINDS OF TESTS

Tests are used for purposes other than measuring knowledge and ability to perform specified duties. For some positions, it is equally important to test ability to make adjustments to new situations or to profit from training. In others, basic mental abilities not dependent on information are essential. Questions which test these things may not appear as pertinent to the duties of the position as those which test for knowledge and information. Yet they are often highly important parts of a fair examination. For very general questions, it is almost impossible to help you direct your study efforts. What we can do is to point out some of the more common of these general abilities needed in public service positions and describe some typical questions.

1) General information

Broad, general information has been found useful for predicting job success in some kinds of work. This is tested in a variety of ways, from vocabulary lists to questions about current events. Basic background in some field of work, such as sociology or economics, may be sampled in a group of questions. Often these are principles which have become familiar to most persons through exposure rather than through formal training. It is difficult to advise you how to study for these questions; being alert to the world around you is our best suggestion.

2) Verbal ability

An example of an ability needed in many positions is verbal or language ability. Verbal ability is, in brief, the ability to use and understand words. Vocabulary and grammar tests are typical measures of this ability. Reading comprehension or paragraph interpretation questions are common in many kinds of civil service tests. You are given a paragraph of written material and asked to find its central meaning.

3) Numerical ability

Number skills can be tested by the familiar arithmetic problem, by checking paired lists of numbers to see which are alike and which are different, or by interpreting charts and graphs. In the latter test, a graph may be printed in the test booklet which you are asked to use as the basis for answering questions.

4) Observation

A popular test for law-enforcement positions is the observation test. A picture is shown to you for several minutes, then taken away. Questions about the picture test your ability to observe both details and larger elements.

5) Following directions

In many positions in the public service, the employee must be able to carry out written instructions dependably and accurately. You may be given a chart with several columns, each column listing a variety of information. The questions require you to carry out directions involving the information given in the chart.

6) Skills and aptitudes

Performance tests effectively measure some manual skills and aptitudes. When the skill is one in which you are trained, such as typing or shorthand, you can practice. These tests are often very much like those given in business school or high school courses. For many of the other skills and aptitudes, however, no short-time preparation can be made. Skills and abilities natural to you or that you have developed throughout your lifetime are being tested.

Many of the general questions just described provide all the data needed to answer the questions and ask you to use your reasoning ability to find the answers. Your best preparation for these tests, as well as for tests of facts and ideas, is to be at your physical and mental best. You, no doubt, have your own methods of getting into an exam-taking mood and keeping "in shape." The next section lists some ideas on this subject.

IV. KINDS OF QUESTIONS

Only rarely is the "essay" question, which you answer in narrative form, used in civil service tests. Civil service tests are usually of the short-answer type. Full instructions for answering these questions will be given to you at the examination. But in case this is your first experience with short-answer questions and separate answer sheets, here is what you need to know:

1) Multiple-choice Questions

Most popular of the short-answer questions is the "multiple choice" or "best answer" question. It can be used, for example, to test for factual knowledge, ability to solve problems or judgment in meeting situations found at work.

A multiple-choice question is normally one of three types—

- It can begin with an incomplete statement followed by several possible endings. You are to find the one ending which *best* completes the statement, although some of the others may not be entirely wrong.
- It can also be a complete statement in the form of a question which is answered by choosing one of the statements listed.

- It can be in the form of a problem – again you select the best answer.

Here is an example of a multiple-choice question with a discussion which should give you some clues as to the method for choosing the right answer:

When an employee has a complaint about his assignment, the action which will *best* help him overcome his difficulty is to
- A. discuss his difficulty with his coworkers
- B. take the problem to the head of the organization
- C. take the problem to the person who gave him the assignment
- D. say nothing to anyone about his complaint

In answering this question, you should study each of the choices to find which is best. Consider choice "A" – Certainly an employee may discuss his complaint with fellow employees, but no change or improvement can result, and the complaint remains unresolved. Choice "B" is a poor choice since the head of the organization probably does not know what assignment you have been given, and taking your problem to him is known as "going over the head" of the supervisor. The supervisor, or person who made the assignment, is the person who can clarify it or correct any injustice. Choice "C" is, therefore, correct. To say nothing, as in choice "D," is unwise. Supervisors have and interest in knowing the problems employees are facing, and the employee is seeking a solution to his problem.

2) True/False Questions

The "true/false" or "right/wrong" form of question is sometimes used. Here a complete statement is given. Your job is to decide whether the statement is right or wrong.

SAMPLE: A roaming cell-phone call to a nearby city costs less than a non-roaming call to a distant city.

This statement is wrong, or false, since roaming calls are more expensive.

This is not a complete list of all possible question forms, although most of the others are variations of these common types. You will always get complete directions for answering questions. Be sure you understand *how* to mark your answers – ask questions until you do.

V. RECORDING YOUR ANSWERS

Computer terminals are used more and more today for many different kinds of exams.

For an examination with very few applicants, you may be told to record your answers in the test booklet itself. Separate answer sheets are much more common. If this separate answer sheet is to be scored by machine – and this is often the case – it is highly important that you mark your answers correctly in order to get credit.

An electronic scoring machine is often used in civil service offices because of the speed with which papers can be scored. Machine-scored answer sheets must be marked with a pencil, which will be given to you. This pencil has a high graphite content which responds to the electronic scoring machine. As a matter of fact, stray dots may register as answers, so do not let your pencil rest on the answer sheet while you are pondering the correct answer. Also, if your pencil lead breaks or is otherwise defective, ask for another.

Since the answer sheet will be dropped in a slot in the scoring machine, be careful not to bend the corners or get the paper crumpled.

The answer sheet normally has five vertical columns of numbers, with 30 numbers to a column. These numbers correspond to the question numbers in your test booklet. After each number, going across the page are four or five pairs of dotted lines. These short dotted lines have small letters or numbers above them. The first two pairs may also have a "T" or "F" above the letters. This indicates that the first two pairs only are to be used if the questions are of the true-false type. If the questions are multiple choice, disregard the "T" and "F" and pay attention only to the small letters or numbers.

Answer your questions in the manner of the sample that follows:

32. The largest city in the United States is
    A. Washington, D.C.
    B. New York City
    C. Chicago
    D. Detroit
    E. San Francisco

1) Choose the answer you think is best. (New York City is the largest, so "B" is correct.)
2) Find the row of dotted lines numbered the same as the question you are answering. (Find row number 32)
3) Find the pair of dotted lines corresponding to the answer. (Find the pair of lines under the mark "B.")
4) Make a solid black mark between the dotted lines.

VI. BEFORE THE TEST

Common sense will help you find procedures to follow to get ready for an examination. Too many of us, however, overlook these sensible measures. Indeed, nervousness and fatigue have been found to be the most serious reasons why applicants fail to do their best on civil service tests. Here is a list of reminders:

- Begin your preparation early – Don't wait until the last minute to go scurrying around for books and materials or to find out what the position is all about.
- Prepare continuously – An hour a night for a week is better than an all-night cram session. This has been definitely established. What is more, a night a week for a month will return better dividends than crowding your study into a shorter period of time.
- Locate the place of the exam – You have been sent a notice telling you when and where to report for the examination. If the location is in a different town or otherwise unfamiliar to you, it would be well to inquire the best route and learn something about the building.
- Relax the night before the test – Allow your mind to rest. Do not study at all that night. Plan some mild recreation or diversion; then go to bed early and get a good night's sleep.
- Get up early enough to make a leisurely trip to the place for the test – This way unforeseen events, traffic snarls, unfamiliar buildings, etc. will not upset you.
- Dress comfortably – A written test is not a fashion show. You will be known by number and not by name, so wear something comfortable.

- Leave excess paraphernalia at home – Shopping bags and odd bundles will get in your way. You need bring only the items mentioned in the official notice you received; usually everything you need is provided. Do not bring reference books to the exam. They will only confuse those last minutes and be taken away from you when in the test room.
- Arrive somewhat ahead of time – If because of transportation schedules you must get there very early, bring a newspaper or magazine to take your mind off yourself while waiting.
- Locate the examination room – When you have found the proper room, you will be directed to the seat or part of the room where you will sit. Sometimes you are given a sheet of instructions to read while you are waiting. Do not fill out any forms until you are told to do so; just read them and be prepared.
- Relax and prepare to listen to the instructions
- If you have any physical problem that may keep you from doing your best, be sure to tell the test administrator. If you are sick or in poor health, you really cannot do your best on the exam. You can come back and take the test some other time.

VII. AT THE TEST

The day of the test is here and you have the test booklet in your hand. The temptation to get going is very strong. Caution! There is more to success than knowing the right answers. You must know how to identify your papers and understand variations in the type of short-answer question used in this particular examination. Follow these suggestions for maximum results from your efforts:

1) Cooperate with the monitor

The test administrator has a duty to create a situation in which you can be as much at ease as possible. He will give instructions, tell you when to begin, check to see that you are marking your answer sheet correctly, and so on. He is not there to guard you, although he will see that your competitors do not take unfair advantage. He wants to help you do your best.

2) Listen to all instructions

Don't jump the gun! Wait until you understand all directions. In most civil service tests you get more time than you need to answer the questions. So don't be in a hurry. Read each word of instructions until you clearly understand the meaning. Study the examples, listen to all announcements and follow directions. Ask questions if you do not understand what to do.

3) Identify your papers

Civil service exams are usually identified by number only. You will be assigned a number; you must not put your name on your test papers. Be sure to copy your number correctly. Since more than one exam may be given, copy your exact examination title.

4) Plan your time

Unless you are told that a test is a "speed" or "rate of work" test, speed itself is usually not important. Time enough to answer all the questions will be provided, but this does not mean that you have all day. An overall time limit has been set. Divide the total time (in minutes) by the number of questions to determine the approximate time you have for each question.

5) Do not linger over difficult questions

If you come across a difficult question, mark it with a paper clip (useful to have along) and come back to it when you have been through the booklet. One caution if you do this – be sure to skip a number on your answer sheet as well. Check often to be sure that you have not lost your place and that you are marking in the row numbered the same as the question you are answering.

6) Read the questions

Be sure you know what the question asks! Many capable people are unsuccessful because they failed to *read* the questions correctly.

7) Answer all questions

Unless you have been instructed that a penalty will be deducted for incorrect answers, it is better to guess than to omit a question.

8) Speed tests

It is often better NOT to guess on speed tests. It has been found that on timed tests people are tempted to spend the last few seconds before time is called in marking answers at random – without even reading them – in the hope of picking up a few extra points. To discourage this practice, the instructions may warn you that your score will be "corrected" for guessing. That is, a penalty will be applied. The incorrect answers will be deducted from the correct ones, or some other penalty formula will be used.

9) Review your answers

If you finish before time is called, go back to the questions you guessed or omitted to give them further thought. Review other answers if you have time.

10) Return your test materials

If you are ready to leave before others have finished or time is called, take ALL your materials to the monitor and leave quietly. Never take any test material with you. The monitor can discover whose papers are not complete, and taking a test booklet may be grounds for disqualification.

VIII. EXAMINATION TECHNIQUES

1) Read the general instructions carefully. These are usually printed on the first page of the exam booklet. As a rule, these instructions refer to the timing of the examination; the fact that you should not start work until the signal and must stop work at a signal, etc. If there are any *special* instructions, such as a choice of questions to be answered, make sure that you note this instruction carefully.

2) When you are ready to start work on the examination, that is as soon as the signal has been given, read the instructions to each question booklet, underline any key words or phrases, such as *least, best, outline, describe* and the like. In this way you will tend to answer as requested rather than discover on reviewing your paper that you *listed without describing*, that you selected the *worst* choice rather than the *best* choice, etc.

3) If the examination is of the objective or multiple-choice type – that is, each question will also give a series of possible answers: A, B, C or D, and you are called upon to select the best answer and write the letter next to that answer on your answer paper – it is advisable to start answering each question in turn. There may be anywhere from 50 to 100 such questions in the three or four hours allotted and you can see how much time would be taken if you read through all the questions before beginning to answer any. Furthermore, if you come across a question or group of questions which you know would be difficult to answer, it would undoubtedly affect your handling of all the other questions.

4) If the examination is of the essay type and contains but a few questions, it is a moot point as to whether you should read all the questions before starting to answer any one. Of course, if you are given a choice – say five out of seven and the like – then it is essential to read all the questions so you can eliminate the two that are most difficult. If, however, you are asked to answer all the questions, there may be danger in trying to answer the easiest one first because you may find that you will spend too much time on it. The best technique is to answer the first question, then proceed to the second, etc.

5) Time your answers. Before the exam begins, write down the time it started, then add the time allowed for the examination and write down the time it must be completed, then divide the time available somewhat as follows:
    - If 3-1/2 hours are allowed, that would be 210 minutes. If you have 80 objective-type questions, that would be an average of 2-1/2 minutes per question. Allow yourself no more than 2 minutes per question, or a total of 160 minutes, which will permit about 50 minutes to review.
    - If for the time allotment of 210 minutes there are 7 essay questions to answer, that would average about 30 minutes a question. Give yourself only 25 minutes per question so that you have about 35 minutes to review.

6) The most important instruction is to *read each question* and make sure you know what is wanted. The second most important instruction is to *time yourself properly* so that you answer every question. The third most important instruction is to *answer every question*. Guess if you have to but include something for each question. Remember that you will receive no credit for a blank and will probably receive some credit if you write something in answer to an essay question. If you guess a letter – say "B" for a multiple-choice question – you may have guessed right. If you leave a blank as an answer to a multiple-choice question, the examiners may respect your feelings but it will not add a point to your score. Some exams may penalize you for wrong answers, so in such cases *only*, you may not want to guess unless you have some basis for your answer.

7) Suggestions
    a. Objective-type questions
        1. Examine the question booklet for proper sequence of pages and questions
        2. Read all instructions carefully
        3. Skip any question which seems too difficult; return to it after all other questions have been answered
        4. Apportion your time properly; do not spend too much time on any single question or group of questions

5. Note and underline key words – *all, most, fewest, least, best, worst, same, opposite*, etc.
6. Pay particular attention to negatives
7. Note unusual option, e.g., unduly long, short, complex, different or similar in content to the body of the question
8. Observe the use of "hedging" words – *probably, may, most likely*, etc.
9. Make sure that your answer is put next to the same number as the question
10. Do not second-guess unless you have good reason to believe the second answer is definitely more correct
11. Cross out original answer if you decide another answer is more accurate; do not erase until you are ready to hand your paper in
12. Answer all questions; guess unless instructed otherwise
13. Leave time for review

b. Essay questions
   1. Read each question carefully
   2. Determine exactly what is wanted. Underline key words or phrases.
   3. Decide on outline or paragraph answer
   4. Include many different points and elements unless asked to develop any one or two points or elements
   5. Show impartiality by giving pros and cons unless directed to select one side only
   6. Make and write down any assumptions you find necessary to answer the questions
   7. Watch your English, grammar, punctuation and choice of words
   8. Time your answers; don't crowd material

8) Answering the essay question

Most essay questions can be answered by framing the specific response around several key words or ideas. Here are a few such key words or ideas:

M's: manpower, materials, methods, money, management
P's: purpose, program, policy, plan, procedure, practice, problems, pitfalls, personnel, public relations

   a. Six basic steps in handling problems:
      1. Preliminary plan and background development
      2. Collect information, data and facts
      3. Analyze and interpret information, data and facts
      4. Analyze and develop solutions as well as make recommendations
      5. Prepare report and sell recommendations
      6. Install recommendations and follow up effectiveness

   b. Pitfalls to avoid
      1. *Taking things for granted* – A statement of the situation does not necessarily imply that each of the elements is necessarily true; for example, a complaint may be invalid and biased so that all that can be taken for granted is that a complaint has been registered

2. *Considering only one side of a situation* – Wherever possible, indicate several alternatives and then point out the reasons you selected the best one
3. *Failing to indicate follow up* – Whenever your answer indicates action on your part, make certain that you will take proper follow-up action to see how successful your recommendations, procedures or actions turn out to be
4. *Taking too long in answering any single question* – Remember to time your answers properly

IX. AFTER THE TEST

Scoring procedures differ in detail among civil service jurisdictions although the general principles are the same. Whether the papers are hand-scored or graded by machine we have described, they are nearly always graded by number. That is, the person who marks the paper knows only the number – never the name – of the applicant. Not until all the papers have been graded will they be matched with names. If other tests, such as training and experience or oral interview ratings have been given, scores will be combined. Different parts of the examination usually have different weights. For example, the written test might count 60 percent of the final grade, and a rating of training and experience 40 percent. In many jurisdictions, veterans will have a certain number of points added to their grades.

After the final grade has been determined, the names are placed in grade order and an eligible list is established. There are various methods for resolving ties between those who get the same final grade – probably the most common is to place first the name of the person whose application was received first. Job offers are made from the eligible list in the order the names appear on it. You will be notified of your grade and your rank as soon as all these computations have been made. This will be done as rapidly as possible.

People who are found to meet the requirements in the announcement are called "eligibles." Their names are put on a list of eligible candidates. An eligible's chances of getting a job depend on how high he stands on this list and how fast agencies are filling jobs from the list.

When a job is to be filled from a list of eligibles, the agency asks for the names of people on the list of eligibles for that job. When the civil service commission receives this request, it sends to the agency the names of the three people highest on this list. Or, if the job to be filled has specialized requirements, the office sends the agency the names of the top three persons who meet these requirements from the general list.

The appointing officer makes a choice from among the three people whose names were sent to him. If the selected person accepts the appointment, the names of the others are put back on the list to be considered for future openings.

That is the rule in hiring from all kinds of eligible lists, whether they are for typist, carpenter, chemist, or something else. For every vacancy, the appointing officer has his choice of any one of the top three eligibles on the list. This explains why the person whose name is on top of the list sometimes does not get an appointment when some of the persons lower on the list do. If the appointing officer chooses the second or third eligible, the No. 1 eligible does not get a job at once, but stays on the list until he is appointed or the list is terminated.

X. HOW TO PASS THE INTERVIEW TEST

The examination for which you applied requires an oral interview test. You have already taken the written test and you are now being called for the interview test – the final part of the formal examination.

You may think that it is not possible to prepare for an interview test and that there are no procedures to follow during an interview. Our purpose is to point out some things you can do in advance that will help you and some good rules to follow and pitfalls to avoid while you are being interviewed.

What is an interview supposed to test?

The written examination is designed to test the technical knowledge and competence of the candidate; the oral is designed to evaluate intangible qualities, not readily measured otherwise, and to establish a list showing the relative fitness of each candidate – as measured against his competitors – for the position sought. Scoring is not on the basis of "right" and "wrong," but on a sliding scale of values ranging from "not passable" to "outstanding." As a matter of fact, it is possible to achieve a relatively low score without a single "incorrect" answer because of evident weakness in the qualities being measured.

Occasionally, an examination may consist entirely of an oral test – either an individual or a group oral. In such cases, information is sought concerning the technical knowledges and abilities of the candidate, since there has been no written examination for this purpose. More commonly, however, an oral test is used to supplement a written examination.

Who conducts interviews?

The composition of oral boards varies among different jurisdictions. In nearly all, a representative of the personnel department serves as chairman. One of the members of the board may be a representative of the department in which the candidate would work. In some cases, "outside experts" are used, and, frequently, a businessman or some other representative of the general public is asked to serve. Labor and management or other special groups may be represented. The aim is to secure the services of experts in the appropriate field.

However the board is composed, it is a good idea (and not at all improper or unethical) to ascertain in advance of the interview who the members are and what groups they represent. When you are introduced to them, you will have some idea of their backgrounds and interests, and at least you will not stutter and stammer over their names.

What should be done before the interview?

While knowledge about the board members is useful and takes some of the surprise element out of the interview, there is other preparation which is more substantive. It *is* possible to prepare for an oral interview – in several ways:

1) Keep a copy of your application and review it carefully before the interview

This may be the only document before the oral board, and the starting point of the interview. Know what education and experience you have listed there, and the sequence and dates of all of it. Sometimes the board will ask you to review the highlights of your experience for them; you should not have to hem and haw doing it.

2) Study the class specification and the examination announcement

Usually, the oral board has one or both of these to guide them. The qualities, characteristics or knowledges required by the position sought are stated in these documents. They offer valuable clues as to the nature of the oral interview. For example, if the job involves supervisory responsibilities, the announcement will usually indicate that knowledge of modern supervisory methods and the qualifications of the candidate as a supervisor will be tested. If so, you can expect such questions, frequently in the form of a hypothetical situation which you are expected to solve. NEVER go into an oral without knowledge of the duties and responsibilities of the job you seek.

3) Think through each qualification required

Try to visualize the kind of questions you would ask if you were a board member. How well could you answer them? Try especially to appraise your own knowledge and background in each area, *measured against the job sought*, and identify any areas in which you are weak. Be critical and realistic – do not flatter yourself.

4) Do some general reading in areas in which you feel you may be weak

For example, if the job involves supervision and your past experience has NOT, some general reading in supervisory methods and practices, particularly in the field of human relations, might be useful. Do NOT study agency procedures or detailed manuals. The oral board will be testing your understanding and capacity, not your memory.

5) Get a good night's sleep and watch your general health and mental attitude

You will want a clear head at the interview. Take care of a cold or any other minor ailment, and of course, no hangovers.

What should be done on the day of the interview?

Now comes the day of the interview itself. Give yourself plenty of time to get there. Plan to arrive somewhat ahead of the scheduled time, particularly if your appointment is in the fore part of the day. If a previous candidate fails to appear, the board might be ready for you a bit early. By early afternoon an oral board is almost invariably behind schedule if there are many candidates, and you may have to wait. Take along a book or magazine to read, or your application to review, but leave any extraneous material in the waiting room when you go in for your interview. In any event, relax and compose yourself.

The matter of dress is important. The board is forming impressions about you – from your experience, your manners, your attitude, and your appearance. Give your personal appearance careful attention. Dress your best, but not your flashiest. Choose conservative, appropriate clothing, and be sure it is immaculate. This is a business interview, and your appearance should indicate that you regard it as such. Besides, being well groomed and properly dressed will help boost your confidence.

Sooner or later, someone will call your name and escort you into the interview room. *This is it.* From here on you are on your own. It is too late for any more preparation. But remember, you asked for this opportunity to prove your fitness, and you are here because your request was granted.

What happens when you go in?

The usual sequence of events will be as follows: The clerk (who is often the board stenographer) will introduce you to the chairman of the oral board, who will introduce you to the other members of the board. Acknowledge the introductions before you sit down. Do not be surprised if you find a microphone facing you or a stenotypist sitting by. Oral interviews are usually recorded in the event of an appeal or other review.

Usually the chairman of the board will open the interview by reviewing the highlights of your education and work experience from your application – primarily for the benefit of the other members of the board, as well as to get the material into the record. Do not interrupt or comment unless there is an error or significant misinterpretation; if that is the case, do not hesitate. But do not quibble about insignificant matters. Also, he will usually ask you some question about your education, experience or your present job – partly to get you to start talking and to establish the interviewing "rapport." He may start the actual questioning, or turn it over to one of the other members. Frequently, each member undertakes the questioning on a particular area, one in which he is perhaps most competent, so you can expect each member to participate in the examination. Because time is limited, you may also expect some rather abrupt switches in the direction the questioning takes, so do not be upset by it. Normally, a board member will not pursue a single line of questioning unless he discovers a particular strength or weakness.

After each member has participated, the chairman will usually ask whether any member has any further questions, then will ask you if you have anything you wish to add. Unless you are expecting this question, it may floor you. Worse, it may start you off on an extended, extemporaneous speech. The board is not usually seeking more information. The question is principally to offer you a last opportunity to present further qualifications or to indicate that you have nothing to add. So, if you feel that a significant qualification or characteristic has been overlooked, it is proper to point it out in a sentence or so. Do not compliment the board on the thoroughness of their examination – they have been sketchy, and you know it. If you wish, merely say, "No thank you, I have nothing further to add." This is a point where you can "talk yourself out" of a good impression or fail to present an important bit of information. Remember, *you close the interview yourself*.

The chairman will then say, "That is all, Mr. _____, thank you." Do not be startled; the interview is over, and quicker than you think. Thank him, gather your belongings and take your leave. Save your sigh of relief for the other side of the door.

How to put your best foot forward

Throughout this entire process, you may feel that the board individually and collectively is trying to pierce your defenses, seek out your hidden weaknesses and embarrass and confuse you. Actually, this is not true. They are obliged to make an appraisal of your qualifications for the job you are seeking, and they want to see you in your best light. Remember, they must interview all candidates and a non-cooperative candidate may become a failure in spite of their best efforts to bring out his qualifications. Here are 15 suggestions that will help you:

1) Be natural – Keep your attitude confident, not cocky

If you are not confident that you can do the job, do not expect the board to be. Do not apologize for your weaknesses, try to bring out your strong points. The board is interested in a positive, not negative, presentation. Cockiness will antagonize any board member and make him wonder if you are covering up a weakness by a false show of strength.

2) Get comfortable, but don't lounge or sprawl

Sit erectly but not stiffly. A careless posture may lead the board to conclude that you are careless in other things, or at least that you are not impressed by the importance of the occasion. Either conclusion is natural, even if incorrect. Do not fuss with your clothing, a pencil or an ashtray. Your hands may occasionally be useful to emphasize a point; do not let them become a point of distraction.

3) Do not wisecrack or make small talk

This is a serious situation, and your attitude should show that you consider it as such. Further, the time of the board is limited – they do not want to waste it, and neither should you.

4) Do not exaggerate your experience or abilities

In the first place, from information in the application or other interviews and sources, the board may know more about you than you think. Secondly, you probably will not get away with it. An experienced board is rather adept at spotting such a situation, so do not take the chance.

5) If you know a board member, do not make a point of it, yet do not hide it

Certainly you are not fooling him, and probably not the other members of the board. Do not try to take advantage of your acquaintanceship – it will probably do you little good.

6) Do not dominate the interview

Let the board do that. They will give you the clues – do not assume that you have to do all the talking. Realize that the board has a number of questions to ask you, and do not try to take up all the interview time by showing off your extensive knowledge of the answer to the first one.

7) Be attentive

You only have 20 minutes or so, and you should keep your attention at its sharpest throughout. When a member is addressing a problem or question to you, give him your undivided attention. Address your reply principally to him, but do not exclude the other board members.

8) Do not interrupt

A board member may be stating a problem for you to analyze. He will ask you a question when the time comes. Let him state the problem, and wait for the question.

9) Make sure you understand the question

Do not try to answer until you are sure what the question is. If it is not clear, restate it in your own words or ask the board member to clarify it for you. However, do not haggle about minor elements.

10) Reply promptly but not hastily

A common entry on oral board rating sheets is "candidate responded readily," or "candidate hesitated in replies." Respond as promptly and quickly as you can, but do not jump to a hasty, ill-considered answer.

11) Do not be peremptory in your answers

A brief answer is proper – but do not fire your answer back. That is a losing game from your point of view. The board member can probably ask questions much faster than you can answer them.

12) Do not try to create the answer you think the board member wants

He is interested in what kind of mind you have and how it works – not in playing games. Furthermore, he can usually spot this practice and will actually grade you down on it.

13) Do not switch sides in your reply merely to agree with a board member

Frequently, a member will take a contrary position merely to draw you out and to see if you are willing and able to defend your point of view. Do not start a debate, yet do not surrender a good position. If a position is worth taking, it is worth defending.

14) Do not be afraid to admit an error in judgment if you are shown to be wrong

The board knows that you are forced to reply without any opportunity for careful consideration. Your answer may be demonstrably wrong. If so, admit it and get on with the interview.

15) Do not dwell at length on your present job

The opening question may relate to your present assignment. Answer the question but do not go into an extended discussion. You are being examined for a *new* job, not your present one. As a matter of fact, try to phrase ALL your answers in terms of the job for which you are being examined.

Basis of Rating

Probably you will forget most of these "do's" and "don'ts" when you walk into the oral interview room. Even remembering them all will not ensure you a passing grade. Perhaps you did not have the qualifications in the first place. But remembering them will help you to put your best foot forward, without treading on the toes of the board members.

Rumor and popular opinion to the contrary notwithstanding, an oral board wants you to make the best appearance possible. They know you are under pressure – but they also want to see how you respond to it as a guide to what your reaction would be under the pressures of the job you seek. They will be influenced by the degree of poise you display, the personal traits you show and the manner in which you respond.

ABOUT THIS BOOK

This book contains tests divided into Examination Sections. Go through each test, answering every question in the margin. We have also attached a sample answer sheet at the back of the book that can be removed and used. At the end of each test look at the answer key and check your answers. On the ones you got wrong, look at the right answer choice and learn. Do not fill in the answers first. Do not memorize the questions and answers, but understand the answer and principles involved. On your test, the questions will likely be different from the samples. Questions are changed and new ones added. If you understand these past questions you should have success with any changes that arise. Tests may consist of several types of questions. We have additional books on each subject should more study be advisable or necessary for you. Finally, the more you study, the better prepared you will be. This book is intended to be the last thing you study before you walk into the examination room. Prior study of relevant texts is also recommended. NLC publishes some of these in our Fundamental Series. Knowledge and good sense are important factors in passing your exam. Good luck also helps. So now study this Passbook, absorb the material contained within and take that knowledge into the examination. Then do your best to pass that exam.

EXAMINATION SECTION

EXAMINATION SECTION
TEST 1

DIRECTIONS: Each question or incomplete statement is followed by several suggested answers or completions. Select the one that BEST answers the question or completes the statement. *PRINT THE LETTER OF THE CORRECT ANSWER IN THE SPACE AT THE RIGHT.*

1. A stenographer can BEST deal with the situation which arises when her pencil breaks during dictation by

    A. asking the person dictating to lend her one
    B. going back to her desk to secure another one
    C. being equipped at every dictation with several pencils
    D. making a call to the supply room for some pencils

    1.____

2. Accuracy is of greater importance than speed in filing CHIEFLY because

    A. city offices have a tremendous amount of filing to do
    B. fast workers are usually inferior workers
    C. there is considerable difficulty in locating materials which have been filed incorrectly
    D. there are many varieties of filing systems which may be used

    2.____

3. Many persons dictate so rapidly that they pay little attention to matters of punctuation and English, but they expect their stenographers to correct errors. This statement implies MOST clearly that stenographers should be

    A. able to write acceptable original reports when required
    B. good citizens as well as good stenographers
    C. efficient clerks as well as good stenographers
    D. efficient in language usage

    3.____

4. A typed letter should resemble a picture properly framed. This statement MOST emphasizes

    A. accuracy   B. speed
    C. convenience   D. neatness

    4.____

5. Of the following, the CHIEF advantage of the use of a mechanical check is that it

    A. guards against tearing in handling the check
    B. decreases the possibility of alteration in the amount of the check
    C. tends to prevent the mislaying and loss of checks
    D. facilitates keeping checks in proper order for mailing

    5.____

6. Of the following, the CHIEF advantage of the use of a dictating machine is that the

    A. stenographer must be able to take rapid dictation
    B. person dictating tends to make few errors
    C. dictator may be dictating letters while the stenographer is busy at some other task
    D. usual noise in an office is lessened

    6.____

7. The CHIEF value of indicating enclosures beneath the identification marks on the lower left side of a letter is that it

    A. acts as a check upon the contents before mailing and upon receiving a letter
    B. helps determine the weight for mailing
    C. is useful in checking the accuracy of typed matter
    D. requires an efficient mailing clerk

8. The one of the following which is NOT an advantage of the window envelope is that it

    A. saves time since the inside address serves also as an outside address
    B. gives protection to the address from wear and tear of the mails
    C. lessens the possibility of mistakes since the address is written only once
    D. tends to be much easier to seal than the plain envelope

9. A question as to proper syllabication of a word at the end of a line may BEST be settled by consulting

    A. the person who dictated the letter
    B. a shorthand manual
    C. a dictionary
    D. a file of letters

10. Mailing a letter which contains many erasures is UNDESIRABLE chiefly because

    A. paper should not be wasted
    B. some stenographers are able to carry on some of the correspondence in an office without consulting their superiors
    C. correspondence should be neat
    D. erasures indicate that the dictator was not certain of what he intended to say in the letter

11. Systematizing for efficiency means MOST NEARLY

    A. performing an assignment despite all interruptions
    B. leaving difficult assignments until the next day
    C. having a definite time schedule for certain daily duties
    D. trying to do as few letters a day as possible

12. The CHIEF value of good paragraphing is that

    A. it is an aid to the stenographer because it shortens letters
    B. the stenographer who uses it will make few errors in her letters
    C. it saves time for the typist
    D. it aids the reader in understanding the whole letter

13. If postage stamps or seals are so placed on a parcel post package that they seal it against inspection, the package must be sent as _____ mail.

    A. first class
    B. second class
    C. third class
    D. special delivery

14. The emergency relief bureau was especially designed to aid   14.____

    A. the needy unemployed
    B. homeless men
    C. homeowners unable to keep up with mortgage payments
    D. needy persons from other parts of the country who had come in search of a job

15. In many cities, immense expense is incurred in straightening streets, removing buildings, and cutting new streets to relieve traffic congestion, filling in and beautifying river and lake fronts, and building parks and playgrounds in places convenient for the people. The necessity of this type of expense is BEST avoided by   15.____

    A. planning
    B. reducing expenditures
    C. a central bureau for purchasing and spending
    D. appropriate changes in the tax rate

16. The city charter operates for the city in somewhat the SAME fashion as   16.____

    A. the United States Supreme Court functions with regard to federal legislation
    B. the United States Constitution operates for the entire country
    C. the Governor functions for the state
    D. P.R. operates in the city

17. The municipal employee should be interested in the activities of the United States Supreme Court PRIMARILY because   17.____

    A. its decisions provide certain kinds of important general rules
    B. the Supreme Court consists of nine persons appointed by the President
    C. the American Constitution is the finest document which man has ever produced
    D. the President's plan for reorganization of the court may be revived

18. Of the following, it is most frequently argued that labor problems are of concern to the municipal employee PRIMARILY because   18.____

    A. the problems of labor are the same as the problems of municipal government
    B. newspapers carry considerable information about labor problems
    C. the municipal employee is a wage or salary earner
    D. a municipal government is of the people, for the people, and by the people

19. Warfare in any part of the world should be of interest to the municipal employee PRIMARILY as a result of the fact that   19.____

    A. strict American neutrality is secured by not permitting the sale of munitions to any country at war
    B. war has not been declared though warfare is raging
    C. the United States frequently participates in the meetings of the United Nations
    D. facilities for transportation and communication have produced a *smaller* world

20. The city regulates certain aspects of housing CHIEFLY because   20.____

    A. the city is the largest municipality in the country
    B. zoning is the concern of all residents of the city

C. housing affects health
D. the state Constitution makes regulation optional

21. In general, it is probably true that the functions which the city administers are those
    A. most necessary to the preservation of the well-being of its residents
    B. of little or no interest to private business
    C. forbidden to the state
    D. not capable of being financed by private business

22. The one of the following which is NOT a regular city department is
    A. Public Welfare   B. Libraries
    C. Purchase   D. Sanitation

23. The present outlook on social work has become different _____ that of the past.
    A. by   B. to   C. with   D. from

KEY (CORRECT ANSWERS)

1. C	11. C
2. C	12. D
3. D	13. A
4. D	14. A
5. B	15. A
6. C	16. B
7. A	17. A
8. D	18. C
9. C	19. D
10. C	20. C

21. A
22. B
23. D

TEST 2

DIRECTIONS: Each question or incomplete statement is followed by several suggested answers or completions. Select the one that BEST answers the question or completes the statement. *PRINT THE LETTER OF THE CORRECT ANSWER IN THE SPACE AT THE RIGHT.*

1. *Re* is MOST frequently read as the abbreviation for 1.____

   A. in regard to B. real estate
   C. receipt D. return enclosure

2. *Prox.* is MOST frequently read as the abbreviation for 2.____

   A. approximate balance B. last month
   C. next month D. by proxy

3. In alphabetical filing, abbreviations such as *Wm.* or *Chas.* are 3.____

   A. disregarded entirely
   B. treated as if spelled out
   C. disregarded except for first letter
   D. placed in parentheses and disregarded

4. Confusion regarding the exact location of certain papers missing from files can probably BEST be avoided by 4.____

   A. using colored tabs
   B. using the Dewey Decimal System
   C. making files available to few persons
   D. consistently using *out* guides

5. On payment of proper fees, special handling is given to _____ mail. 5.____

   A. all B. first class
   C. second class D. fourth class

6. The MAXIMUM weight of packages which can be sent by fourth class mail is _____ pounds. 6.____

   A. 70 B. 50 C. 100 D. 25

7. The CHIEF advantage of a night letter over a telegram is probably 7.____

   A. speed B. economy
   C. brevity D. dependability

8. The regular monthly rate charged for telephone service pays for all 8.____

   A. outgoing calls made during the month
   B. outgoing local calls up to a certain number
   C. calls including a stated number of out-of-town calls
   D. calls except out-of-town calls

9. Property tax is computed on 9.____

   A. actual value B. purchase price
   C. assessed valuation D. amount of first mortgage

10. The abbreviation *N.B.* means

    A. disregard
    B. no good
    C. does not belong
    D. note carefully

11. Of the following, the one which is NOT one of the values of the typewritten signature in a business letter is that the

    A. receiver can read the typewritten signature if the ink signature is not legible
    B. typewritten signature leaves a record on carbon copies for a reference regarding signer
    C. signer may simply initial above the typewritten signature if he so desires
    D. typewritten signature indicates that the contents of the letter have been checked by the sender

12. There is no more convincing mark of a cultured speaker or writer than accuracy of statement.
    This statement stressed the importance of

    A. new ideas
    B. facts
    C. acquiring a pleasing speaking voice
    D. poise

13. When a department is called, the voice which answers the telephone is, to the person calling, the department itself. This statement implies MOST clearly that

    A. only one person should answer the telephone in each office
    B. a clerk with a pleasing, courteous telephone manner is an asset to an office
    C. an efficient clerk will terminate all telephone conversations as quickly as possible
    D. making personal telephone calls is looked upon with disfavor in some offices

14. Probably the CHIEF advantage of filling higher vacancies by promotion is that this procedure

    A. stimulates the worker to improve his work and general knowledge and technique
    B. provides an easy check on the work of the individual
    C. eliminates personnel problems in a department
    D. harmonizes the work of one department with that of all other departments

15. Greatest efficiency is reached when filing method and filing clerk are harmoniously adjusted to the needs of an office.
    This statement means MOST NEARLY that

    A. the filing method is more important than the clerk in securing the successful handling of valuable papers
    B. almost any clerk can do office filing well
    C. a good clerk using a good filing system assures good filing
    D. every office needs a filing system

KEY (CORRECT ANSWERS)

1. A
2. C
3. B
4. D
5. D

6. A
7. B
8. B
9. C
10. D

11. D
12. B
13. B
14. A
15. C

TEST 3

DIRECTIONS: Each question or incomplete statement is followed by several suggested answers or completions. Select the one that BEST answers the question or completes the statement. *PRINT THE LETTER OF THE CORRECT ANSWER IN THE SPACE AT THE RIGHT.*

1. Your superior, Mr. Hotchkiss, is in conference and has requested that he not be disturbed.
   The condition under which you would MOST probably disturb the conference is:

   A. A Mr. Smith, whom you have not seen before, says he has important business with Mr. Hotchkiss
   B. Mrs. Hotchkiss telephones, saying there has been a serious accident at home
   C. You do not know how a certain letter should be filed and wish to ask the advice of Mr. Hotchkiss
   D. A fellow clerk wishes to ask Mr. Hotchkiss whether a particular city department handles certain matters

   1._____

2. Your superior directs you to find certain papers. You know the purpose for which the papers are to be used. In the course of your search for the papers, you come across certain material which would be very useful for the purpose to be served by the papers. You should

   A. bring the papers to your superior and ask whether he wants the other materials
   B. go to your superior immediately and ask whether he wishes both the materials and the papers or only one of the two
   C. bring to your superior the other materials together with the papers you were directed to find
   D. bring only the other materials to your superior and point out the manner in which these materials are of greater value than the papers

   2._____

3. If a fellow employee asks you a question to which you do not know the answer, you should say,

   A. I don't know. What's the difference?
   B. The answer to that question forms no part of my duties here.
   C. My dear sir, the thing for you to do is to look the matter up yourself because it is your responsibility, not mine.
   D. I'm sorry. I don't know.

   3._____

4. In general, it is probably true that MOST people are

   A. so self-seeking that they pay no attention to the wants, needs, or behavior of others
   B. so changeable that one never knows what his fellow employee is likely to do next
   C. not worth the trouble to bother about
   D. quite ready to help others

   4._____

5. Of the following, the one which is NOT a reason for avoiding clerical errors is that

   A. time is lost
   B. money is wasted

   5._____

C. many clerks are very intelligent
D. serious consequences may follow

6. Of the following, the MAIN reason for keeping a careful record of incoming mail is that

   A. some people are less industrious than others
   B. this record helps to speed up outgoing mail
   C. this record is a kind of legal evidence
   D. this information may be useful in answering questions which may arise

7. Of the following, the MAIN reason for using a calculating machine is that

   A. a lesser knowledge of arithmetic is needed
   B. a more attractive product is obtained
   C. greater speed and accuracy are obtained
   D. it is not difficult to learn how to operate a calculating machine

8. Of the following, the MAIN reason for being polite over the telephone is that

   A. persons who are speaking over the telephone cannot see each other
   B. politeness makes for pleasant business relationships
   C. it is not at all difficult or costly to be courteous
   D. one's voice is of great importance because voice reflects mood

9. Because telephone directories contain printed pages, they are called books. This statement assumes MOST NEARLY that

   A. some books do not contain printed pages
   B. not all telephone directories are books which contain printed pages
   C. material which contains printed pages is called a book
   D. all books which contain printed pages are called telephone directories

10. Mr. Cross must be using a budget because he has been able to reduce his unnecessary expenses.
    On the basis of only the material included in this statement, it may MOST accurately be said that this statement assumes that

    A. all people who use budgets lower certain types of expenses
    B. some people who do not use budgets reduce unnecessary expenses
    C. some people who use budgets do not reduce unnecessary expenses
    D. all types of expenses are reduced by the use of a budget

11. Of the following, the MAIN purpose of tabulating a set of figures is that

    A. interpretation is facilitated
    B. computational accuracy is assured
    C. pictorial representations lend themselves to easy evaluation
    D. any set of figures must be based upon prior arithmetical calculations

12. Of the following, the LEAST important characteristic of a good tabular presentation of data is that

    A. decimals are rounded off to the nearest whole number
    B. the title appears at the top

C. entries are correct
D. the title is brief

13. To print tabular material is always much more expensive than to print straight text. It follows MOST NEARLY that

   A. the more columns and subdivisions there are in a table, the more expensive is the printing
   B. the omission of the number and title from a table greatly reduces the expense of printing
   C. it is always desirable to substitute text for tabular material
   D. a graphic presentation should almost always be substituted for a table in order to save money

14. The circumstances under which a person-to-person telephone call should be made occur when the person calling

   A. wishes to make the least expensive type of telephone call
   B. is certain that the person to be called is at his desk waiting for the call
   C. believes that the person to be called is not likely to be present to receive the call
   D. is seeking information which is probably known by all the members of an office, rather than only a single person

15. A check which customarily states on its face the purpose for which the money is paid is MOST probably termed a _____ check.

   A. certified   B. cashier's
   C. voucher   D. personal

KEY (CORRECT ANSWERS)

1. B
2. C
3. D
4. D
5. C
6. D
7. C
8. B
9. C
10. A
11. A
12. A
13. A
14. C
15. C

TEST 4

DIRECTIONS: Each question or incomplete statement is followed by several suggested answers or completions. Select the one that BEST answers the question or completes the statement. *PRINT THE LETTER OF THE CORRECT ANSWER IN THE SPACE AT THE RIGHT.*

1. The BEST arrangement of folder tabs for easy location of material in the files is

    A. staggered from left to right
    B. zigzagged in alternate positions
    C. staggered from right to left
    D. placed in one center position, one tab directly behind the other

2. Generally speaking (without regard to special localities where there might be a preponderance of like names), the letter in the alphabet requiring the MOST captions for guides in a breakdown or division of the alphabet is the letter

    A. B   B. C   C. M   D. S

3. In filing terminology, coding means

    A. making a preliminary arrangement of names according to caption before bringing them together in final order of arrangement
    B. reading correspondence and determining the proper caption under which it is to be filed
    C. marking a card or paper with symbols or other means of identification to indicate where it is to be placed in the files according to a predetermined plan
    D. placing a card or paper in the files showing where correspondence may be located under another name or title

4. A duplex-number system of filing is a(n)

    A. decimal system
    B. arrangement of guides and folders with a definite color scheme to aid in filing and locating material
    C. system of filing by which classified subjects are divided and subdivided by number for the purpose of expansion
    D. method of filing names according to sound instead of spelling

Questions 5-7.

DIRECTIONS: Questions 5 through 7 are to be answered SOLELY on the basis of information contained in the following passage.

It is common knowledge that ability to do a particular job and performance on the job do not always go hand in hand. Persons with great potential abilities sometimes fall down on the job because of laziness or lack of interest in the job, while persons with mediocre talents have often achieved excellent results through their industry and their loyalty to the interests of their employers. It is clear, therefore, that in a balanced personnel program, measures of employee ability need to be supplemented by measures of employee performance, for the final test of any employee is his performance on the job.

5. The MOST accurate of the following statements, on the basis of the above paragraph, is that

   A. employees who lack ability are usually not industrious
   B. an employee's attitudes are more important than his abilities
   C. mediocre employees who are interested in their work are preferable to employees who possess great ability
   D. superior capacity for performance should be supplemented with proper attitudes

6. On the basis of the above paragraph, the employee of most value to his employer is NOT necessarily the one who

   A. best understands the significance of his duties
   B. achieves excellent results
   C. possesses the greatest talents
   D. produces the greatest amount of work

7. According to the above paragraph, an employee's efficiency is BEST determined by an

   A. appraisal of his interest in his work
   B. evaluation of the work performed by him
   C. appraisal of his loyalty to his employer
   D. evaluation of his potential ability to perform his work

8. A clerk interested in world affairs should know that UNESCO is concerned MAINLY with international cooperation

   A. in the control of atomic power
   B. in the relocation of refugees
   C. to raise health standards throughout the world
   D. through the free exchange of information on education, art, and science

9. The one of the following which is NOT a power of the New York City Council is

   A. investigation through a special committee of any matters relating to the property of the City
   B. fixing of the tax rate
   C. adoption of the expense budget
   D. authorization of all franchises

10. Assume that one of your duties as a clerk is to keep a constantly changing mailing list up to date.
    Of the following, the BEST method for you to follow is to use a(n)

    A. alphabetical card index with loose cards, one for each name
    B. bound volume with a separate page or group of pages for each letter
    C. loose-leaf notebook with names beginning with the same letter listed on the same sheet or group of sheets
    D. typed list, add names at end of the list, and retype periodically in proper alphabetical order

11. In evaluating the effectiveness of a filing system, the one of the following criteria which you should consider MOST important is the

    A. safety of material in the event of a fire
    B. ease with which material may be located
    C. quantity of papers which can be filed
    D. extent to which material in the filing systems is being used

11.____

12. A set of cards numbered from 1 to 300 has been filed in numerical order in such a way that the highest number is at the front of the file and lowest number is at the rear. It is desired that the cards be reversed to run in ascending order.
    The BEST of the following methods that can be used in performing this task is to begin at the

    A. front of the file and remove the cards one at a time, placing each one face up on top of the one removed before
    B. front of the file and remove the cards one at a time, placing each one face down on top of the one removed before
    C. back of the file and remove the cards in small groups, placing each group face down on top of the group removed before
    D. back of the file and remove the cards one at a time, placing each one face up on top of the one removed before

12.____

13. Assume you are the receptionist for Mr. Brown, an official in your department. It is your duty to permit only persons having important business to see this official; otherwise, you are to refer them to other members of the staff. A man tells you that he must see Mr. Brown on a very urgent and confidential matter. He gives you his name and says that Mr. Brown knows him, but he does not wish to tell you the nature of the matter.
    Of the following, the BEST action for you to take under these circumstances is to

    A. permit this man to see Mr. Brown without further question, since the matter seems to be urgent
    B. refer this man to another member of the staff, since Mr. Brown may not wish to see him
    C. call Mr. Brown and explain the situation to him, and ask him whether he wishes to see this man
    D. tell this man that you will permit him to see Mr. Brown only if he informs you of the nature of his business

13.____

14. You are given copies of an important official notice together with a memorandum stating that each of the employees listed on the memorandum is to receive a copy of the official notice.
    In order to have definite proof that each of the employees listed has received a copy of the notice, the BEST of the following courses of action for you to take as you hand the notice to each of the employees is to

    A. put your initials next to the employee's name on the memorandum
    B. ask the employee to sign the notice you have given him in your presence
    C. have the employee put his signature next to his name on the memorandum
    D. ask the employee to read the notice in your presence

14.____

4 (#4)

15. The Mayor of the City of New York is elected for a term of _____ years.   15.____
    A. 2   B. 3   C. 4   D. 5

KEY (CORRECT ANSWERS)

1. A   6. C
2. D   7. B
3. C   8. D
4. C   9. D
5. D   10. A

11. B
12. A
13. C
14. C
15. C

TEST 5

DIRECTIONS: Each question or incomplete statement is followed by several suggested answers or completions. Select the one that BEST answers the question or completes the statement. *PRINT THE LETTER OF THE CORRECT ANSWER IN THE SPACE AT THE RIGHT.*

1. When an employee is encouraged by his supervisor to think of new ideas in connection with his work, the habit of improving work methods is fostered.
   The one of the following which the MOST valid implication of the above statement is that

   A. the improvement of work methods should be the concern not only of the supervisor but of the employee as well
   B. an employee without initiative cannot perform his job well
   C. an employee may waste too much time in experimenting with new work methods
   D. an improved method for performing a task should not be used without the approval of the supervisor

   1.____

2. The report on the work of the three employees furnishes definite proof that Jones is more efficient than Smith, and that Brown is less efficient than Jones.
   On the basis of the above information, the MOST accurate of the following statements is that

   A. Brown is more efficient than Smith
   B. Smith is more efficient than Brown
   C. Smith is not necessarily less efficient than Jones
   D. Brown is not necessarily more efficient than Smith

   2.____

3. The Dewey Decimal System is used MOST widely in

   A. government offices   B. private offices
   C. social welfare organizations   D. libraries

   3.____

4. Provision for handling a letter from a utility company marked *the first of next month* would necessitate that the letter be placed in a _____ file.

   A. follow-up   B. numeric   C. subject   D. geographic

   4.____

5. The SIMPLEST system of filing is

   A. subject   B. geographic   C. alphabetic   D. numeric

   5.____

6. Almost all students with a high school average of 80% or over were admitted to the college.
   On the basis of this statement, it would be MOST accurate to assume that

   A. a high school average of *80%* or over was required for admittance to the college
   B. some students with a high school average of less than 80% were admitted to the college
   C. a high school average of at least 80% was desirable but not necessary for admission to the college
   D. some students with a high school average of at least 80% were not admitted to the college

   6.____

15

7. Suppose that you are filing a large number of cards. Your supervisor asks you to interrupt your work, arrange a group of letters alphabetically by name of writer, and then file the letters in a correspondence file. He asks, however, that you show the letters to him before you file them. You finish alphabetizing the letters in a few minutes, but your supervisor is not available.
Of the following, the BEST action for you to take is to

   A. file the letters as you have been directed, provided that your work has been checked by at least one other clerk
   B. file the letters as directed by your supervisor and explain to him when he returns the reason for your action
   C. wait at your supervisor's desk until he returns and you have an opportunity to show the letters to him
   D. resume filing cards until you have an opportunity to show the letters to your supervisor

8. The supervisor of a large central bureau is responsible for the accuracy of the work performed by her subordinates. The total number of errors made during the month indicates, in a general way, whether the work has been performed with reasonable accuracy. However, this is not in itself a true measure, but must be considered in relation to the total volume of work produced.
On the basis of this statement, the accuracy of work performed in a central typing bureau is MOST truly measured by the

   A. total number of errors made during a specified period
   B. comparison of the number of errors made during one month with the number made during the preceding month
   C. ratio between the number of errors made and the quantity of work produced during the month
   D. average amount of work produced by the unit during each month

9. As a clerk assigned to keeping payroll records in your department, you are instructed by your supervisor to use a new method for keeping the records. You think that the new method will be less effective than the one you are now using.
In this situation, it would be MOST advisable for you to

   A. use the new method to keep the records even if you think it may be less effective
   B. continue to use the method you consider to be more effective without saying anything to your supervisor
   C. use the method you consider to be more effective and then tell your supervisor your reasons for doing so
   D. use the new method only if you can improve its effectiveness

10. The term of office of a United States Senator is _____ years.
    A. 8   B. 6   C. 4   D. 2

11. Employees are required NOT to smoke in file rooms principally because
    A. they might interfere with the rights of others working in the same area
    B. of the danger of cancer
    C. of the narrow areas of the file room
    D. of the danger of fire

12. The MAIN reason a city employee should be polite is that 12._____

    A. he may get into trouble if he is not polite
    B. he never knows when he may be talking to a city official
    C. politeness is a duty which any city employee owes the public
    D. politeness will make him appear to be alert and efficient

13. In the United States, there is no 13._____

    A. general sales tax
    B. state income tax
    C. state compulsory automobile inspection
    D. state compulsory automobile insurance

14. It is LEAST correct to say that the commissioners of the various city departments are 14._____

    A. appointed by the mayor and may usually be removed by him at will
    B. generally part-time officials and serve without pay
    C. responsible for submitting regular reports to the mayor on the operations of their departments
    D. the top policy-making officials in these departments

15. The form of government under which the city of New York functions is known as the 15._____

    A. Commision-Mayor   B. Council-Manager
    C. Master-Plan   D. Mayor-Council

KEY (CORRECT ANSWERS)

1. A
2. D
3. D
4. A
5. D

6. D
7. D
8. C
9. A
10. B

11. D
12. C
13. A
14. B
15. D

EXAMINATION SECTION
TEST 1

DIRECTIONS: Each question or incomplete statement is followed by several suggested answers or completions. Select the one that BEST answers the question or completes the statement. *PRINT THE LETTER OF THE CORRECT ANSWER IN THE SPACE AT THE RIGHT.*

1. If you open a personal letter by mistake, the one of the following actions which it would generally be BEST for you to take is to

    A. ignore your error, attach the envelope to the letter, and distribute in the usual manner
    B. personally give the addressee the letter without any explanation
    C. place the letter inside the envelope, indicate under your initials that it was opened in error, and give to the addressee
    D. reseal the envelope or place the contents in another envelope and pass on to addressee

    1.____

2. If you receive a telephone call regarding a matter which your office does not handle, you should FIRST

    A. give the caller the telephone number of the proper office so that he can dial again
    B. offer to transfer the caller to the proper office
    C. suggest that the caller re-dial since he probably dialed incorrectly
    D. tell the caller he has reached the wrong office and then hang up

    2.____

3. When you answer the telephone, the MOST important reason for identifying yourself and your organization is to

    A. give the caller time to collect his or her thoughts
    B. impress the caller with your courtesy
    C. inform the caller that he or she has reached the right number
    D. set a business-like tone at the beginning of the conversation

    3.____

4. The one of the following cases in which you would NOT place a special notation in the left margin of a letter that you have typed is when

    A. one of the copies is intended for someone other than the addressee of the letter
    B. you enclose a flyer with the letter
    C. you sign your superior's name to the letter, at his or her request
    D. the letter refers to something being sent under separate cover

    4.____

5. Suppose that you accidentally cut a letter or enclosure as you are opening an envelope with a paper knife.
   The one of the following that you should do FIRST is to

    A. determine whether the document is important
    B. clip or staple the pieces together and process as usual
    C. mend the cut document with transparent tape
    D. notify the sender that the communication was damaged and request another copy

    5.____

19

6. As soon as you pick up the phone, a very angry caller begins immediately to complain about city agencies and *red tape*. He says that he has been shifted to two or three different offices. It turns out that he is seeking information which is not immediately available to you. You believe you know, however, where it can be found.
Which of the following actions is the BEST one for you to take?

   A. To eliminate all confusion, suggest that the caller write the mayor stating explicitly what he wants.
   B. Apologize by telling the caller how busy city agencies now are, but also tell him directly that you do not have the information he needs.
   C. Ask for the caller's telephone number, and assure him you will call back after you have checked further.
   D. Give the caller the name and telephone number of the person who might be able to help, but explain that you are not positive he will get results.

7. Suppose that one of your duties is to dictate responses to routine requests from the public for information. A letter writer asks for information which, as expressed in a one-sentence, explicit agency rule, cannot be given out to the public.
Of the following ways of answering the letter, which is the MOST efficient?

   A. Quote verbatim that section of the agency rules which prohibits giving this information to the public.
   B. Without quoting the rule, explain why you cannot accede to the request and suggest alternative sources.
   C. Describe how carefully the request was considered before classifying it as subject to the rule forbidding the issuance of such information.
   D. Acknowledge receipt of the letter and advise that the requested information is not released to the public.

8. Suppose you assist in supervising a staff which has rather high morale, and your own supervisor asks you to poll the staff to find out who will be able to work overtime this particular evening to help complete emergency work.
Which of the following approaches would be MOST likely to win their cooperation while maintaining their morale?

   A. Tell them that the better assignments will be given only to those who work overtime.
   B. Tell them that occasional overtime is a job requirement.
   C. Assure them they'll be doing you a personal favor.
   D. Let them know clearly why the overtime is needed.

9. Suppose that you have been asked to write and to prepare for reproduction new departmental vacation leave regulations.
After you have written the new regulations, all of which fit on two pages, which one of the following would be the BEST method of reproducing 1,000 copies?

   A. An outside private printer because you can best maintain confidentiality using this technique
   B. Photocopying because the copies will have the best possible appearance
   C. Sending the file to all department employees as printable PDFs
   D. Printing and collating on the office high-volume printer

10. You are in charge of verifying employees' qualifications. This involves telephoning previous employers and schools. One of the applications which you are reviewing contains information which you are almost certain is correct on the basis of what the employee has told you.
    The BEST thing to do is to

    A. check the information again with the employer
    B. perform the required verification procedures
    C. accept the information as valid
    D. ask a superior to verify the information

11. The practice of immediately identifying oneself and one's place of employment when contacting persons on the telephone is

    A. *good* because the receiver of the call can quickly identify the caller and establish a frame of reference
    B. *good* because it helps to set the caller at ease with the other party
    C. *poor* because it is not necessary to divulge that information when making general calls
    D. *poor* because it takes longer to arrive at the topic to be discussed

12. Which one of the following should be the MOST important overall consideration when preparing a recommendation to automate a large-scale office activity?
    The

    A. number of models of automated equipment available
    B. benefits and costs of automation
    C. fears and resistance of affected employees
    D. experience of offices which have automated similar activities

13. A tickler file is MOST appropriate for filing materials

    A. chronologically according to date they were received
    B. alphabetically by name
    C. alphabetically by subject
    D. chronologically according to date they should be followed up

14. Which of the following is the BEST reason for decentralizing rather then centralizing the use of duplicating machines?

    A. Developing and retaining efficient duplicating machine operators
    B. Facilitating supervision of duplicating services
    C. Motivating employees to produce legible duplicated copies
    D. Placing the duplicating machines where they are most convenient and most frequently used

15. Window envelopes are sometimes considered preferable to individually addressed envelopes PRIMARILY because

    A. window envelopes are available in standard sizes for all purposes
    B. window envelopes are more attractive and official-looking
    C. the use of window envelopes eliminates the risk of inserting a letter in the wrong envelope
    D. the use of window envelopes requires neater typing

16. In planning the layout of a new office, the utilization of space and the arrangement of staff, furnishings, and equipment should usually be MOST influenced by the

    A. gross square footage
    B. status differences in the chain of command
    C. framework of informal relationships among employees
    D. activities to be performed

17. Office forms sometimes consist of several copies, each of a different color. The MAIN reason for using different colors is to

    A. make a favorable impression on the users of the form
    B. distinguish each copy from the others
    C. facilitate the preparation of legible carbon copies
    D. reduce cost, since using colored stock permits recycling of paper

18. Which of the following is the BEST justification for obtaining a photocopying machine for the office?

    A. A photocopying machine can produce an unlimited number of copies at a low fixed cost per copy.
    B. Employees need little training in operating a photocopying machine.
    C. Office costs will be reduced and efficiency increased.
    D. The legibility of a photocopy generally is superior to copy produced by any other office duplicating device.

19. An administrative officer in charge of a small fund for buying office supplies has just written a check to Charles Laird, a supplier, and has sent the check by messenger to him. A half-hour later, the messenger telephones the administrative officer. He has lost the check.
    Which of the following is the MOST important action for the administrative officer to take under these circumstances?

    A. Ask the messenger to return and write a report describing the loss of the check.
    B. Make a note on the performance record of the messenger who lost the check.
    C. Take the necessary steps to have payment stopped on the check.
    D. Refrain from doing anything since the check may be found shortly.

20. A petty cash fund is set up PRIMARILY to

    A. take care of small investments that must be made from time to time
    B. take care of small expenses that arise from time to time
    C. provide a fund to be used as the office wants to use it with little need to maintain records
    D. take care of expenses that develop during emergencies such as machine breakdowns and fires

21. Your superior has asked you to send a package from your agency to a government agency in another city. He has written out the message and has indicated the name of the government agency.
    When you prepare the package for mailing, which of the following items that your superior has not mentioned must you be sure to include?

A. Today's date
B. The full address of the government agency
C. A polite opening such as *Dear Sirs*
D. A final sentence such as *We would appreciate hearing from your agency in reply as soon as is convenient for you*

22. In addition to the original piece of correspondence, one should USUALLY also have typed

    A. a single copy
    B. as many copies as can be typed at one time
    C. no more copies than are needed
    D. two copies

23. The one of the following which is the BEST procedure to follow when making a short insert in a completed dictation is to

    A. label the insert with a letter and indicate the position of the insert in the text by writing the identifying letter in the proper place
    B. squeeze the insert into its proper place within the main text of the dictation
    C. take down the insert and check the placement with the person who dictated when you are ready to transcribe your notes
    D. transcribe the dictation into longhand, including the insert in its proper position

24. The one of the following procedures which will be MOST efficient in helping you to quickly open your dictation notebook to a clean sheet is to

    A. clip or place a rubberband around the used portion of the notebook
    B. leave the book out and open to a clean page when not in use
    C. transcribe each dictation after it is given and rip out the used pages
    D. use a book marker to indicate which portion of the notebook has been used

25. The purpose of dating your dictation notebooks is GENERALLY to

    A. enable you to easily refer to your notes at a later date
    B. ensure that you transcribe your notes in the order in which they were dictated
    C. set up a precise record-keeping procedure
    D. show your employer that you pay attention to detail

KEY (CORRECT ANSWERS)

1. C
2. B
3. C
4. C
5. C

6. C
7. A
8. D
9. D
10. B

11. A
12. B
13. D
14. D
15. C

16. D
17. B
18. C
19. C
20. B

21. B
22. C
23. A
24. A
25. A

TEST 2

DIRECTIONS: Each question or incomplete statement is followed by several suggested answers or completions. Select the one that BEST answers the question or completes the statement. *PRINT THE LETTER OF THE CORRECT ANSWER IN THE SPACE AT THE RIGHT.*

1. With regard to typed correspondence received by most offices, which of the following is the GREATEST problem?

    A. Verbosity
    B. Illegibility
    C. Improper folding
    D. Excessive copies

2. Of the following, the GREATEST advantage of flash drives over rewritable CD storage is that they

    A. are portable
    B. are both smaller and lighter
    C. contain more storage space
    D. allow files to be deleted to free space

3. Suppose that a large quantity of information is in the files which are located a good distance from your desk. Almost every worker in your office must use these files constantly. Your duties in particular require that you daily refer to about 25 of the same items. They are short, one-page items distributed throughout the files. In this situation, your BEST course would be to

    A. take the items that you use daily from the files and keep them on your desk, inserting *out cards* in their place
    B. go to the files each time you need the information so that the items will be there when other workers need them
    C. make xerox copies of the information you use most frequently and keep them in your desk for ready reference
    D. label the items you use most often with different colored tabs for immediate identification

4. Of the following, the MOST important advantage of preparing manuals of office procedures in loose-leaf form is that this form

    A. permits several employees to use different sections simultaneously
    B. facilitates the addition of new material and the removal of obsolete material
    C. is more readily arranged in alphabetical order
    D. reduces the need for cross-references to locate material carried under several headings

5. Suppose that you establish a new clerical procedure for the unit you supervise. Your keeping a close check on the time required by your staff to handle the new procedure is WISE mainly because such a check will find out

    A. whether your subordinates know how to handle the new procedure
    B. whether a revision of the unit's work schedule will be necessary as a result of the new procedure
    C. what attitude your employees have toward the new procedure
    D. what alterations in job descriptions will be necessitated by the new procedure

6. The numbered statements below relate to the stenographic skill of taking dictation. According to authorities on secretarial practices, which of these are generally recommended guides to development of efficient stenographic skills?

STATEMENTS
1. A stenographer should date her notebook daily to facilitate locating certain notes at a later time.
2. A stenographer should make corrections of grammatical mistakes while her boss is dictating to her.
3. A stenographer should draw a line through the dictated matter in her notebook after she has transcribed it.
4. A stenographer should write in longhand unfamiliar names and addresses dictated to her.

The CORRECT answer is:

A. Only Statements 1, 2, and 3 are generally recommended guides.
B. Only Statements 2, 3, and 4 are generally recommended guides.
C. Only Statements 1, 3, and 4 are generally recommended guides.
D. All four statements are generally recommended guides.

7. According to generally recognized rules of filing in an alphabetic filing system, the one of the following names which normally should be filed LAST is

A. Department of Education, New York State
B. F.B.I.
C. Police Department of New York City
D. P.S. 81 of New York City

8. Which one of the following forms for the typed name of the dictator in the closing lines of a letter is generally MOST acceptable in the United States?

A. (Dr.) James F. Fenton
B. Dr. James F. Fenton
C. Mr. James F. Fenton, Ph.D.
D. James F. Fenton

9. Which of the following is, MOST generally, a rule to be followed when typing a rough draft?

A. The copy should be single spaced.
B. The copy should be triple spaced.
C. There is no need for including footnotes.
D. Errors must be neatly corrected.

10. An office assistant needs a synonym.
Of the following, the book which she would find MOST useful is

A. a world atlas
B. BARTLETT'S FAMILIAR QUOTATIONS
C. a manual of style
D. a thesaurus

11. Of the following examples of footnotes, the one that is expressed in the MOST generally accepted standard form is: 11._____

   A. Johnson, T.F. (Dr.), English for Everyone, 3rd or 4th edition; New York City Linton Publishing Company, p. 467
   B. Frank Taylor, English for Today (New York: Rayton Publishing Company, 1971), p. 156
   C. Ralph Wilden, English for Tomorrow, Reynolds Publishing Company, England, p. 451
   D. Quinn, David, Yesterday's English (New York: Baldwin Publishing Company, 1972), p. 431

12. Standard procedures are used in offices PRIMARILY because 12._____

   A. an office is a happier place if everyone is doing the tasks in the same manner
   B. particular ways of doing jobs are considered more efficient than other ways
   C. it is good discipline for workers to follow standard procedures approved by the supervisor
   D. supervisors generally don't want workers to be creative in planning their work

13. Assume that an office assistant has the responsibility for compiling, typing, and mailing a preliminary announcement of Spring term course offerings. The announcement will go to approximately 900 currently enrolled students. Assuming that the following equipment is available for use, the MOST EFFECTIVE method for distributing the announcement to all 900 students is to 13._____

   A. e-mail it as a text document using the electronic student mailing list
   B. post the announcement as a PDF document for download on the department website
   C. send it by fax
   D. post the announcement and leave copies in buildings around campus

14. *Justified typing* is a term that refers MOST specifically to typewriting copy 14._____

   A. that has been edited and for which final copy is being prepared
   B. in a form that allows for an even right-hand margin
   C. with a predetermined vertical placement for each alternate line
   D. that has been approved by the supervisor and his superior

15. Which one of the following is the BEST form for the address in a letter? 15._____

   A. Mr. John Jones
      Vice President, The Universal Printing Company
      1220 Fifth Avenue
      New York, 10023 New York
   B. Mr. John Jones, Vice President
      The Universal Printing Company
      1220 Fifth Avenue
      New York, New York 10023
   C. Mr. John Jones, Vice President, The Universal Printing Company
      1220 Fifth Avenue
      New York, New York 10023

D. Mr. John Jones Vice President,
The Universal Printing Company
1220 Fifth Avenue
New York, 10023 New York

16. Of the following, the CHIEF advantage of the use of window envelopes over ordinary envelopes is that window envelopes

    A. eliminate the need for addressing envelopes
    B. protect the confidential nature of enclosed material
    C. cost less to buy than ordinary envelopes
    D. reduce the danger of the address becoming illegible

17. In the complimentary close of a business letter, the FIRST letter of _____ should be capitalized.

    A. all the words
    B. none of the words
    C. only the first word
    D. only the last word

18. Assume that one of your duties is to procure needed office supplies from the supply room. You are permitted to draw supplies every two weeks.
    The one of the following which would be the MOST desirable practice for you to follow in obtaining supplies is to

    A. obtain a quantity of supplies sufficient to last for several months to make certain that enough supplies are always on hand
    B. determine the minimum supply necessary to keep on hand for the various items and obtain an additional quantity as soon as possible after the supply on hand has been reduced to this minimum
    C. review the supplies once a month to determine what items have been exhausted and obtain an additional quantity as soon as possible
    D. obtain a supply of an item as soon after it has been exhausted as is possible

19. Some offices that keep carbon copies of letters use several different colors of carbon paper for making carbon copies.
    Of the following, the CHIEF reason for using different colors of carbon paper is to

    A. facilitate identification of different types of letters in the files
    B. relieve the monotony of typing and filing carbon copies
    C. reduce the costs of preparing carbon copies
    D. utilize both sides of the carbon paper for typing

20. Your supervisor asks you to post an online ad for freelance designers interested in submitting samples for a new company logo. Prospective workers should be proficient in which of the following software?

    A. Microsoft Word
    B. Adobe Acrobat Pro
    C. Adobe Illustrator
    D. Microsoft PowerPoint

21. Gary Thompson is applying for a position with the firm of Gray and Williams.
    Which letter should be filed in top position in the *Application* folder?

    A. A letter of recommendation written on September 18 by Johnson & Smith
    B. Williams' letter of October 8 requesting further details regarding Thompson's experience

C. Thompson's letter of September 8 making application for a position as sales manager
D. Letter of September 20 from Alfred Jackson recommending Thompson for the job

22. The USUAL arrangement in indexing the names of the First National Bank, Toledo, is   22.____

    A. First National Bank, Toledo, Ohio
    B. Ohio, First National Bank, Toledo
    C. Toledo, First National Bank, Ohio
    D. Ohio, Toledo, First National Bank

23. A single line through typed text indicating that it's incorrect or invalid is known as a(n)   23.____

    A. underline
    B. strikethrough
    C. line font
    D. eraser

24. A typical e-mail with an attachment should contain all of the following for successful transmittal EXCEPT   24.____

    A. recipient's address   B. file attachment
    C. body text   D. description of attachment

25. The subject line in a letter is USUALLY typed a _____ space below the _____.   25.____

    A. single; inside address   B. single; salutation
    C. double; inside address   D. double; salutation

KEY (CORRECT ANSWERS)

1.	A		11.	B
2.	C		12.	B
3.	C		13.	A
4.	B		14.	B
5.	B		15.	B
6.	C		16.	A
7.	D		17.	C
8.	D		18.	B
9.	B		19.	A
10.	D		20.	C

21. B
22. A
23. B
24. D
25. D

EXAMINATION SECTION
TEST 1

DIRECTIONS: Each question or incomplete statement is followed by several suggested answers or completions. Select the one that BEST answers the question or completes the statement. *PRINT THE LETTER OF THE CORRECT ANSWER IN THE SPACE AT THE RIGHT.*

1. A coworker has e-mailed a file containing a spreadsheet for your review. Which of the following programs will open the file?

    A. Adobe Reader
    B. Microsoft Excel
    C. Microsoft PowerPoint
    D. Adobe Illustrator

2. A report needs to be forwarded immediately to a supervisor in another office. Which of the following is the LEAST effective way of giving the supervisor the report?

    A. scanning the report and e-mailing the file
    B. faxing it to the supervisor's office
    C. uploading it to the office network and informing the supervisor
    D. waiting for the supervisor to come to your office and giving it to him/her then

3. Suppose your supervisor is on the telephone in his office and an applicant arrives for a scheduled interview with him.
Of the following, the BEST procedure to follow ordinarily is to

    A. informally chat with the applicant in your office until your supervisor has finished his phone conversation
    B. escort him directly into your supervisor's office and have him wait for him there
    C. inform your supervisor of the applicant's arrival and try to make the applicant feel comfortable while waiting
    D. have him hang up his coat and tell him to go directly in to see your supervisor

Questions 4-9.

DIRECTIONS: Questions 4 through 9 each consist of a sentence which may or may not be an example of good English usage. Consider grammar, punctuation, spelling, capitalization, awkwardness, etc. Examine each sentence, and then choose the correct statement about it from the four choices below it. If the English usage in the sentence given is better than any of the changes suggested in options B, C, or D, choose option A. Do not choose an option that will change the meaning of the sentence.

4. The report, along with the accompanying documents, were submitted for review.

    A. This is an example of acceptable writing.
    B. The words *were submitted* should be changed to *was submitted*.
    C. The word *accompanying* should be spelled *accompaning*.
    D. The comma after the word *report* should be taken out.

5. If others must use your files, be certain that they understand how the system works, but insist that you do all the filing and refiling. 5.____

   A. This is an example of acceptable writing.
   B. There should be a period after the word *works*, and the word *but* should start a new sentence.
   C. The words *filing* and *refiling* should be spelled *fileing* and *refileing*.
   D. There should be a comma after the word *but*.

6. The appeal was not considered because of its late arrival. 6.____

   A. This is an example of acceptable writing.
   B. The word *its* should be changed to *it's*.
   C. The word *its* should be changed to *the*.
   D. The words *late arrival* should be changed to *arrival late*.

7. The letter must be read carefuly to determine under which subject it should be filed. 7.____

   A. This is an example of acceptable writing.
   B. The word *under* should be changed to *at*.
   C. The word *determine* should be spelled *determin*.
   D. The word *carefuly* should be spelled *carefully*.

8. He showed potential as an office manager, but he lacked skill in delegating work. 8.____

   A. This is an example of acceptable writing.
   B. The word *delegating* should be spelled *delagating*.
   C. The word *potential* should be spelled *potencial*.
   D. The words *lie lacked* should be changed to *was lacking*.

9. His supervisor told him that it would be all right to receive personal mail at the office. 9.____

   A. This is an example of acceptable writing.
   B. The words *all right* should be changed to *alright*.
   C. The word *personal* should be spelled *personel*.
   D. The word *mail* should be changed to *letters*.

Questions 10-13.

DIRECTIONS: Questions 10 through 13 are to be answered SOLELY on the basis of the information given in the following passage.

    Typed pages can reflect the simplicity of modern art in a machine age. Lightness and evenness can be achieved by proper layout and balance of typed lines and white space. Instead of solid, cramped masses of uneven, crowded typing, there should be a pleasing balance up and down as well as horizontal.

    To have real balance, your page must have a center. The eyes see the center of the sheet slightly above the real center. This is the way both you and the reader see it. Try imagining a line down the center of the page that divides the paper in equal halves. On either side of your paper, white space and blocks of typing need to be similar in size and shape. Although left and right margins should be equal, top and bottom margins need not be as exact. It looks better to hold a bottom border wider than a top margin, so that your typing rests upon a cushion of white space. To add interest to the appearance of the page, try making one paragraph between one-half and two-thirds the size of an adjacent paragraph.

Thus, by taking full advantage of your typewriter, the pages that you type will not only be accurate but will also be attractive.

10. It can be inferred from the passage that the BASIC importance of proper balancing on a typed page is that proper balancing   10.____

    A. makes a typed page a work of modern art
    B. provides exercise in proper positioning of a typewriter
    C. increases the amount of typed copy on the paper
    D. draws greater attention and interest to the page

11. A reader will tend to see the center of a typed page   11.____

    A. somewhat higher than the true center
    B. somewhat lower than the true center
    C. on either side of the true center
    D. about two-thirds of an inch above the true center

12. Which of the following suggestions is NOT given by the passage?   12.____

    A. Bottom margins may be wider than top borders.
    B. Keep all paragraphs approximately the same size.
    C. Divide your page with an imaginary line down the middle.
    D. Side margins should be equalized.

13. Of the following, the BEST title for this passage is: 13.____

    A. INCREASING THE ACCURACY OF THE TYPED PAGE
    B. DETERMINATION OF MARGINS FOR TYPED COPY
    C. LAYOUT AND BALANCE OF THE TYPED PAGE
    D. HOW TO TAKE FULL ADVANTAGE OF THE TYPEWRITER

14. In order to type addresses on a large number of envelopes MOST efficiently, you should   14.____

    A. insert another envelope into the typewriter before removing each typed envelope
    B. take each typed envelope out of the machine before starting the next envelope
    C. insert several envelopes into the machine at one time, keeping all top and bottom edges even
    D. insert several envelopes into the machine at one time, keeping the top edge of each envelope two inches below the top edge of the one beneath it

15. A senior typist has completed copying a statistical report from a rough draft.
    Of the following, the BEST way to be sure that her typing is correct is for the typist to   15.____

    A. fold the rough draft, line it up with the typed copy, compare one-half of the columns with the original, and have a co-worker compare the other half
    B. check each line of the report as it is typed and then have a co-worker check each line again after the entire report is finished

C. have a co-worker add each column and check the totals on the typed copy with the totals on the original
D. have a co-worker read aloud from the rough draft while the typist checks the typed copy and then have the typist read while the co-worker checks

16. In order to center a heading when typing a report, you should

    A. measure your typing paper with a ruler and begin the heading one-third of the way in from the left margin
    B. begin the heading at the point on the typewriter scale which is 50 minus the number of letters in the heading
    C. multiply the number of characters in the heading by two and begin the heading that number of spaces in from the left margin
    D. begin the heading at the point on the scale which is equal to the center point of your paper minus one-half the number of characters and spaces in the heading

17. Which of the following recommendations concerning the use of copy paper for making typewritten copies should NOT be followed?

    A. Copy papers should be checked for wrinkles before being used.
    B. Legal-size copy paper may be folded if it is too large to fit into a convenient drawer space.
    C. When several sheets of paper are being used, they should be fastened with a paper clip at the top after insertion in the typewriter.
    D. For making many copies, paper of the same weight and brightness should be used.

18. Assume that a new typist, Norma Garcia, has been assigned to work under your supervision and is reporting to work for the first time. You formally introduce Norma to her co-workers and suggest that a few of the other typists explain the office procedures and typing formats to her. The practice of instructing Norma in her duties in this manner is

    A. *good* because she will be made to feel at home
    B. *good* because she will learn more about routine office tasks from co-workers than from you
    C. *poor* because her co-workers will resent the extra work
    D. *poor* because you will not have enough control over her training

19. Suppose that Jean Brown, a typist, is typing a letter following the same format that she has always used. However, she notices that the other two typists in her office are also typing letters, but are using a different format. Jean is concerned that she might not have been informed of a change in format.
Of the following, the FIRST action that Jean should take is to

    A. seek advice from her supervisor as to which format to use
    B. ask the other typists whether she should use a new format for typing letters
    C. disregard the format that the other typists are using and continue to type in the format she had been using
    D. use the format that the other typists are using, assuming that it is a newly accepted method

20. Suppose that the new office to which you have been assigned has put up Christmas decorations, and a Christmas party is being planned by the city agency in which you work. However, nothing has been said about Christmas gifts.
It would be CORRECT for you to assume that

    A. you are expected to give a gift to your supervisor
    B. your supervisor will give you a gift
    C. you are expected to give gifts only to your subordinates
    D. you will neither receive gifts nor will you be expected to give any

20. ____

KEY (CORRECT ANSWERS)

1.	B	11.	A
2.	D	12.	B
3.	C	13.	C
4.	B	14.	A
5.	A	15.	D
6.	A	16.	D
7.	D	17.	B
8.	A	18.	D
9.	A	19.	A
10.	D	20.	D

TEST 2

DIRECTIONS: Each question or incomplete statement is followed by several suggested answers or completions. Select the one that BEST answers the question or completes the statement. *PRINT THE LETTER OF THE CORRECT ANSWER IN THE SPACE AT THE RIGHT.*

1. The supervisor you assist is under great pressure to meet certain target dates. He has scheduled an emergency meeting to take place in a few days, and he asks you to send out notices immediately. As you begin to prepare the notices, however, you realize he has scheduled the meeting for a Saturday, which is not a working day. Also, you sense that your supervisor is not in a good mood.
   Which of the following is the MOST effective method of handling this situation?

   A. Change the meeting date to the first working day after that Saturday and send out the notices.
   B. Change the meeting date to a working day on which his calendar is clear and send out the notices.
   C. Point out to your supervisor that the date is a Saturday.
   D. Send out the notices as they are since you have received specific instructions.

   1.____

Questions 2-7.

DIRECTIONS: Questions 2 through 7 each consist of a sentence which may or may not be an example of good English usage. Consider grammar, punctuation, spelling, capitalization, awkwardness, etc. Examine each sentence, and then choose the correct statement about it from the four choices below it. If the English usage in the sentence given is better than any of the changes suggested in options B, C, or D, choose option A. Do not choose an option that will change the meaning of the sentence.

2. The typist used an extention cord in order to connect her typewriter to the outlet nearest to her desk.

   A. This is an example of acceptable writing.
   B. A period should be placed after the word *cord,* and the word *in* should have a capital I.
   C. A comma should be placed after the word *typewriter.*
   D. The word *extention* should be spelled *extension.*

   2.____

3. He would have went to the conference if he had received an invitation.

   A. This is an example of acceptable writing.
   B. The word *went* should be replaced by the word *gone.*
   C. The word *had* should be replaced by *would have.*
   D. The word *conference* should be spelled *conferance.*

   3.____

4. In order to make the report neater, he spent many hours rewriting it.

   A. This is an example of acceptable writing.
   B. The word *more* should be inserted before the word *neater.*
   C. There should be a colon after the word *neater.*
   D. The word *spent* should be changed to *have spent.*

   4.____

5. His supervisor told him that he should of read the memorandum more carefully. 5._____

   A. This is an example of acceptable writing.
   B. The word *memorandum* should be spelled *memorandom*.
   C. The word *of* should be replaced by the word *have*.
   D. The word *carefully* should be replaced by the word *careful*.

6. It was decided that two separate reports should be written. 6._____

   A. This is an example of acceptable writing.
   B. A comma should be inserted after the word *decided*.
   C. The word *be* should be replaced by the word *been*.
   D. A colon should be inserted after the word *that*.

7. She don't seem to understand that the work must be done as soon as possible. 7._____

   A. This is an example of acceptable writing.
   B. The word *doesn't* should replace the word *don't*.
   C. The word *why* should replace the word *that*.
   D. The word *as* before the word *soon* should be eliminated.

Questions 8-11.

DIRECTIONS: Questions 8 through 11 are to be answered SOLELY on the basis of the following passage.

There is nothing that will take the place of good sense on the part of the stenographer. You may be perfect in transcribing exactly what the dictator says and your speed may be adequate; but without an understanding of the dictator's intent as well as his words, you are likely to be a mediocre secretary.

A serious error that is made when taking dictation is putting down something that does not make sense. Most people who dictate material would rather be asked to repeat and explain than to receive transcribed material which has errors due to inattention or doubt. Many dictators request that their grammar be corrected by their secretaries; but unless specifically asked to do so, secretaries should not do it without first checking with the dictator. Secretaries should be aware that, in some cases, dictators may use incorrect grammar or slang expressions to create a particular effect.

Some people dictate commas, periods, and paragraphs, while others expect the stenographer to know when, where, and how to punctuate. A well-trained secretary should be able to indicate the proper punctuation by listening to the pauses and tones of the dictator's voice.

A stenographer who has taken dictation from the same person for a period of time should be able to understand him under most conditions. By increasing her tact, alertness, and efficiency, a secretary can become more competent.

8. According to the passage, which of the following statements concerning the dictation of punctuation is CORRECT? 8._____
   A

   A. dictator may use incorrect punctuation to create a desired style

B. dictator should indicate all punctuation
C. stenographer should know how to punctuate based on the pauses and tones of the dictator
D. stenographer should not type any punctuation if it has not been dictated to her

9. According to the passage, how should secretaries handle grammatical errors in a dictation?
Secretaries should

   A. *not correct* grammatical errors unless the dictator is aware that this is being done
   B. *correct* grammatical errors by having the dictator repeat the line with proper pauses
   C. *correct* grammatical errors if they have checked the correctness in a grammar book
   D. *correct* grammatical errors based on their own good sense

10. If a stenographer is confused about the method of spacing and indenting of a report which has just been dictated to her, she GENERALLY should

    A. do the best she can
    B. ask the dictator to explain what she should do
    C. try to improve her ability to understand dictated material
    D. accept the fact that her stenographic ability is not adequate

11. In the last line of the first paragraph, the word *mediocre* means MOST NEARLY

    A. superior   B. disregarded
    C. respected   D. second-rate

12. Assume that is is your responsibility to schedule meetings for your supervisor, who believes in starting these meetings strictly on time. He has told you to schedule separate meetings with Mr. Smith and Ms. Jones, which will last approximately 20 minutes each. You have told Mr. Smith to arrive at 10:00 A.M. and Ms. Jones at 10:30 A.M. Your supervisor will have an hour of free time at 11:00 A.M. At 10:25 A.M., Mr. Smith arrives and states that there was a train delay, and he is sorry that he is late. Ms. Jones has not yet arrived. You do not know who Mr. Smith and Ms. Jones are or what the meetings will be about.
Of the following, the BEST course of action for you to take is to

    A. send Mr. Smith in to see your supervisor; and when Ms. Jones arrives, tell her that your supervisor's first meeting will take more time than he expected
    B. tell Mr. Smith that your supervisor has a meeting at 10:30 A.M. and that you will have to reschedule his meeting for another day
    C. check with your supervisor to find out if he would prefer to see Mr. Smith immediately or at 11:00 A.M.
    D. encourage your supervisor to meet with Mr. Smith immediately because Mr. Smith's late arrival was not intentional

13. Assume that you have been told by your boss not to let anyone disturb him for the rest of the afternoon unless absolutely necessary since he has to complete some urgent work. His supervisor, who is the bureau chief, telephones and asks to speak to him.
The BEST course of action for you to take is to

A. ask the bureau chief if he can leave a message
B. ask your boss if he can take the call
C. tell the bureau chief that your boss is out
D. tell your boss that his instructions will get you into trouble

14. Which one of the following is the MOST advisable procedure for a stenographer to follow when a dictator asks her to make extra copies of dictated material?

    A. Note the number of copies required at the beginning of the notes.
    B. Note the number of copies required at the end of the notes.
    C. Make a mental note of the number of copies required to be made.
    D. Make a checkmark beside the notes to serve as a reminder that extra copies are required.

15. Suppose that, as you are taking shorthand notes, the dictator tells you that the sentence he has just dictated is to be deleted.
    Of the following, the BEST thing for you to do is to

    A. place the correction in the left-hand margin next to the deleted sentence
    B. write the word *delete* over the sentence and place the correction on a separate page for corrections
    C. erase the sentence and use that available space for the correction
    D. draw a line through the sentence and begin the correction on the next available line

16. Assume that your supervisor, who normally dictates at a relatively slow rate, begins dictating to you very rapidly. You find it very difficult to keep up at this speed. Which one of the following is the BEST action to take in this situation?

    A. Ask your supervisor to dictate more slowly since you are having difficulty.
    B. Continue to take the dictation at the fast speed and fill in the blanks later.
    C. Interrupt your supervisor with a question about the dictation, hoping that when she begins again it will be slower.
    D. Refuse to take the dictation unless given at the speed indicated in your job description.

17. Assume that you have been asked to put a heading on the second, third, and fourth pages of a four-page letter to make sure they can be identified in case they are separated from the first page.
    Which of the following is it LEAST important to include in such a heading?

    A. Date of the letter
    B. Initials of the typist
    C. Name of the person to whom the letter is addressed
    D. Number of the page

18. Which one of the following is NOT generally accepted when dividing words at the end of a line?
    Dividing

    A. a hyphenated word at the hyphen
    B. a word immediately after the prefix
    C. a word immediately before the suffix
    D. proper names between syllables

19. In the preparation of a business letter which has two enclosures, the MOST generally accepted of the following procedures to follow is to type

   A. *See Attached Items* one line below the last line of the body of the letter
   B. *See Attached Enclosures* to the left of the signature
   C. *Enclosures 2* at the left margin below the signature line
   D. nothing on the letter to indicate enclosures since it will be obvious to the reader that there are enclosures in the envelope

20. Standard rules for typing spacing have developed through usage. According to these rules, one space is left AFTER

   A. a comma
   B. every sentence
   C. a colon
   D. an opening parenthesis

KEY (CORRECT ANSWERS)

1.	C	11.	D
2.	D	12.	C
3.	B	13.	B
4.	A	14.	A
5.	C	15.	D
6.	A	16.	A
7.	B	17.	B
8.	C	18.	D
9.	A	19.	C
10.	B	20.	A

EXAMINATION SECTION

TEST 1

DIRECTIONS: Each question or incomplete statement is followed by several suggested answers or completions. Select the one that BEST answers the question or completes the statement. *PRINT THE LETTER OF THE CORRECT ANSWER IN THE SPACE AT THE RIGHT.*

Questions 1-22.

DIRECTIONS: Read through each group of words. Indicate in the space at the right the letter of the misspelled word.

1. A. miniature   B. recession   1.____
    C. accommodate   D. supress

2. A. mortgage   B. illogical   2.____
    C. fasinate   D. pronounce

3. A. calendar   B. heros   3.____
    C. ecstasy   D. librarian

4. A. initiative   B. extraordinary   4.____
    C. villian   D. exaggerate

5. A. absence   B. sense   5.____
    C. dosn't   D. height

6. A. curiosity   B. ninety   6.____
    C. truely   D. grammar

7. A. amateur   B. definate   7.____
    C. meant   D. changeable

8. A. excellent   B. studioes   8.____
    C. achievement   D. weird

9. A. goverment   B. description   9.____
    C. sergeant   D. desirable

10. A. proceed   B. anxious   10.____
    C. neice   D. precede

11. A. environment   B. omitted   11.____
    C. apparant   D. misconstrue

12. A. comparative   B. hindrance   12.____
    C. benefited   D. unamimous

13. A. embarrass   B. recommend   13._____
    C. desciple   D. argument

14. A. sophomore   B. suprintendent   14._____
    C. concievable D. disastrous

15. A. agressive   B. questionnaire   15._____
    C. occurred   D. rhythm

16. A. peaceable   B. conscientious   16._____
    C. redicule   D. deterrent

17. A. mischievious   B. writing   17._____
    C. competition   D. athletics

18. A. auxiliary   B. synonymous   18._____
    C. maneuver   D. repitition

19. A. existence   B. optomistic   19._____
    C. acquitted   D. tragedy

20. A. hypocrisy   B. parrallel   20._____
    C. exhilaration   D. prevalent

21. A. convalesence   B. infallible   21._____
    C. destitute   D. grotesque

22. A. magnanimity   B. asassination   22._____
    C. incorrigible   D. pestilence

Questions 23-40.

DIRECTIONS: In Questions 23 through 40, one sentence fragment contains an error in punctuation or capitalization. Indicate the letter of the INCORRECT sentence fragment and place it in the space at the right.

23. A. Despite a year's work   23._____
    B. in a well-equipped laboratory
    C. my Uncle failed to complete his research
    D. now he will never graduate.

24. A. Gene, if you are going to sleep   24._____
    B. all afternoon I will enter
    C. that ladies' golf tournament
    D. sponsored by the Chamber of Commerce.

3 (#1)

25. A. Seeing the cat slink toward the barn,
    B. the farmer's wife jumped off the
    C. ladder picked up a broom, and began
    D. shouting at the top of her voice.

26. A. Extending over southeast Idaho and
    B. northwest Wyoming, the Tetons
    C. are noted for their height; however the
    D. highest peak is actually under 14,000 feet.

27. A. "Sarah, can you recall the name
    B. of the English queen
    C. who supposedly said, 'We are not
    D. amused?"

28. A. My aunt's graduation present to me
    B. cost, I imagine more than she could
    C. actually afford. It's a
    D. Swiss watch with numerous features.

29. A. On the left are examples of buildings
    B. from the Classical Period; two temples
    C. one of which was dedicated to Zeus; the
    D. Agora, a marketplace; and a large arch.

30. A. Tired of sonic booms, the people who
    B. live near Springfield's Municipal Airport
    C. formed an anti noise organization
    D. with the amusing name of Sound Off.

31. A. "Joe, Mrs. Sweeney said, "your family
    B. arrives Sunday. Since you'll be in
    C. the Labor Day parade, we could ask Mr.
    D. Krohn, who has a big car, to meet them."

32. A. The plumber emerged from the basement and
    B. said, "Mr. Cohen I found the trouble in
    C. your water heater. Could you move those
    D. Schwinn bikes out of my way?"

33. A. The President walked slowly to the
    B. podium, bowed to Edward Everett Hale
    C. the other speaker, and began his formal address:
    D. "Fourscore and seven years ago...."

34. A. Mr. Fontana, I hope, will arrive before
    B. the beginning of the ceremonies; however,
    C. if his plane is delayed, I have a substitute
    D. speaker who can be here at a moments' notice.

25.____
26.____
27.____
28.____
29.____
30.____
31.____
32.____
33.____
34.____

35. A. Gladys wedding dress, a satin creation,
     B. lay crumpled on the floor; her veil,
     C. torn and streaked, lay nearby. "Jilted!"
     D. shrieked Gladys. She was clearly annoyed.

35.____

36. A. Although it is poor grammar, the word
     B. hopefully has become television's newest
     C. pet expression; I hope (to use the correct
     D. form) that it will soon pass from favor.

36.____

37. A.   Plaza Apartment Hotel
     B.   103 Tower road
     C.   Hampstead, Iowa 52025
     D.   March 13, 2021

37.____

38. A. Circulation Department
     B. British History Illustrated
     C. 3000 Walnut Street
     D. Boulder Colorado 80302

38.____

39. A. Dear Sirs:
     B.   Last spring I ordered a subscription to your
     C. magazine. I had read and enjoyed the May
     D. issue containing the article titled "kings."

39.____

40. A.   I have not however, received a
     B. single issue. Will you check this?
     C.   Sincerely,
     D. Maria Herrera

40.____

Questions 41-70.

DIRECTIONS: Questions 41 through 70 represent common grammatical concerns: subject-verb agreement, appropriate use of pronouns, and appropriate use of verbs. Read each sentence and indicate the letter of the grammatically CORRECT answer in the space at the right.

41. THE REIVERS, one of William Faulkner's last works, _____ made into a movie starring Steve McQueen.
    A. has been   B. have been   C. are being   D. were

41.____

42. He _____ on the ground, his eyes fastened on an ant slowly pushing a morsel of food toward the ant hill.
    A. layed   B. laid   C. had laid   D. lay

42.____

43. Nobody in the tri-cities _____ to admit that a flood could be disastrous.
    A. are willing   B. have been willing
    C. is willing   D. were willing

43.____

44. "_____," the senator asked, "have you convinced to run against the incumbent?"
    A. Who B. Whom C. Whomever D. Womsoever

45. Of all the psychology courses that I took, Statistics 101 _____ the most demanding.
    A. was B. are C. is D. were

46. Neither the conductor nor the orchestra members _____ the music to be applauded so enthusiastically.
    A. were expecting
    B. was expecting
    C. is expected
    D. has been expecting

47. The requirements for admission to the Lettermen's Club _____ posted outside the athletic director's office for months.
    A. was B. was being C. has been D. have been

48. Please give me a list of the people _____ to compete in the kayak race.
    A. whom you think have planned
    B. who you think has planned
    C. who you think is planning
    D. who you think are planning

49. I saw Eloise and Abelard earlier today; _____ were riding around in a fancy 1956 MG.
    A. she and him B. her and him C. she and he D. her and he

50. If you _____ the trunk in the attic, I'll unpack it later today.
    A. can sit
    B. are able to sit
    C. can set
    D. have sat

51. _____ all of the flour been used, or may I borrow three cups?
    A. Have B. Has C. Is D. Could

52. In exasperation, the cycle shop's owner suggested that _____ there too long.
    A. us boys were
    B. we boys were
    C. us boys had been
    D. we boys had been

53. Idleness as well as money _____ the root of all evil.
    A. have been
    B. were to have been
    C. is
    D. are

54. Only the string players from the quartet—Gregory, Isaac, _____—remained after the concert to answer questions.
    A. him, and I
    B. he, and I
    C. him, and me
    D. he, and me

55. Of all the antiques that _____ for sale, Gertrude chose to buy a stupid glass thimble.
    A. was
    B. is
    C. would have
    D. were

56. The detective snapped, "Don't confuse me with theories about _____ you believe committed the crime!"
    A. who B. whom C. whomever D. which

57. _____ when we first called, we might have avoided our present predicament.
    A. The plumber's coming
    B. If the plumber would have come
    C. If the plumber had come
    D. If the plumber was to have come

58. We thought the sun _____ in the north until we discovered that our compass was defective.
    A. had rose
    B. had risen
    C. had rised
    D. had raised

59. Each play of Shakespeare's _____ more than _____ share of memorable characters.
    A. contain its
    B. contains; its
    C. contains; it's
    D. contain; their

60. Our English teacher suggested to _____ seniors that either Tolstoy or Dickens _____ the outstanding novelist of the nineteenth century.
    A. we; was considered
    B. we; were considered
    C. us; was considered
    D. us; were considered

61. Sherlock Holmes, together with his great friend and companion Dr. Watson, _____ to aid the woman _____ had stumbled into the room.
    A. has agreed; who
    B. have agreed; whom
    C. has agreed; whom
    D. have agreed; who

62. Several of the deer _____ when they spotted my backpack _____ open in the meadow.
    A. was frightened; laying
    B. were frightened; lying
    C. were frightened; laying
    D. was frightened; lying

63. After the Scholarship Committee announces _____ selection, hysterics often _____.
    A. it's; occur
    B. its; occur
    C. their; occur
    D. their; occurs

64. I _____ the key on the table last night so you and _____ could find it.
    A. layed; her
    B. lay; she
    C. laid; she
    D. laid; her

65. Some of the antelope _____ wandered away from the meadow where the rancher _____ the block of salt.
    A. has; sat
    B. has; set
    C. have; had set
    D. has; sets

66. Macaroni and cheese _____ best to us (that is, to Andy and _____) when Mother adds extra cheddar cheese.
    A. tastes; I
    B. tastes; me
    C. taste; me
    D. taste; I

66.____

67. Frank said, "It must have been _____ called the phone company."
    A. she who
    B. she whom
    C. her who
    D. her whom

67.____

68. The herd _____ moving restlessly at every bolt of lightning; it was either Ted or _____ who saw the beginning of the stampede.
    A. was; me
    B. were; I
    C. was; I
    D. have been; me

68.____

69. The foreman _____ his lateness by saying that his alarm clock _____ until six minutes before eight.
    A. explains; had not rang
    B. explained; has not rung
    C. has explained; rung
    D. explained; hadn't rung

69.____

70. Of all the coaches, Ms. Cox is the only one who _____ that Sherry dives more gracefully than _____.
    A. is always saying; I
    B. is always saying; me
    C. are always saying; I
    D. were always saying; me

70.____

Questions 71-90.

DIRECTIONS: Choose the word in Questions 71 through 90 that is MOST opposite in meaning to the italicized word.

71. *fact*
    A. statistic
    B. statement
    C. incredible
    D. conjecture

71.____

72. *stiff*
    A. fastidious
    B. babble
    C. supple
    D. apprehensive

72.____

73. *blunt*
    A. concise   B. tactful   C. artistic   D. humble

73.____

74. *foreign*
    A. pertinent   B. comely   C. strange   D. scrupulous

74.____

75. *anger*
    A. infer   B. pacify   C. taint   D. revile

75.____

76. *frank*
    A. earnest   B. reticent   C. post   D. expensive

76.____

77. *secure*
    A. precarious   B. acquire   C. moderate   D. frenzied

78. *petty*
    A. harmonious   B. careful
    C. forthright   D. momentous

79. *concede*
    A. dispute   B. reciprocate
    C. subvert   D. propagate

80. *benefit*
    A. liquidation   B. bazaar
    C. detriment   D. profit

81. *capricious*
    A. preposterous   B. constant
    C. diabolical   D. careless

82. *boisterous*
    A. devious   B. valiant   C. girlish   D. taciturn

83. *harmony*
    A. congruence   B. discord   C. chagrin   D. melody

84. *laudable*
    A. auspicious   B. despicable
    C. acclaimed   D. doubtful

85. *adherent*
    A. partisan   B. stoic   C. renegade   D. recluse

86. *exuberant*
    A. frail   B. corpulent   C. austere   D. bigot

87. *spurn*
    A. accede   B. flail   C. efface   D. annihilate

88. *spontaneous*
    A. hapless   B. corrosive
    C. intentional   D. willful

89. *disparage*
    A. abolish   B. exude   C. incriminate   D. extol

90. *timorous*
    A. succinct   B. chaste   C. audacious   D. insouciant

KEY (CORRECT ANSWERS)

1. D	21. A	41. A	61. A	81. B
2. C	22. B	42. D	62.	82. D
3. B	23. C	43. C	63. B	83. B
4. C	24. B	44. B	64. C	84. B
5. C	25. C	45. A	65. C	85. C
6. C	26. C	46. A	66. B	86. C
7. B	27. D	47. D	67. A	87. A
8. B	28. B	48. A	68. C	88. C
9. A	29. B	49. C	69. D	89. D
10. C	30. C	50. C	70. A	90. C
11. C	31. A	51. B	71. D	
12. D	32. B	52. D	72. C	
13. C	33. B	53. C	73. B	
14. C	34. D	54. B	74. A	
15. A	35. A	55. D	75. B	
16. C	36. B	56. B	76. B	
17. A	37. B	57. C	77. A	
18. D	38. D	58. B	78. D	
19. B	39. D	59. B	79. A	
20. B	40. A	60. C	80. C	

EXAMINATION SECTION
TEST 1

DIRECTIONS: Each question or incomplete statement is followed by several suggested answers or completions. Select the one that BEST answers the question or completes the statement. *PRINT THE LETTER OF THE CORRECT ANSWER IN THE SPACE AT THE RIGHT.*

Questions 1-25. A student has written an article for the high school newspaper, using the skills learned in a stenography and typewriting class in its preparation. In the article which follows, certain words or groups of words are underlined and numbered. The underlined word or group of words may be incorrect because they present an error in grammar, usage, sentence structure, capitalization, diction, or punctuation. For each numbered word or group of words, there is an identically numbered question consisting of four choices based only on the underlined portion. Indicate the BEST choice. <u>Unnecessary changes will be considered incorrect.</u>

TIGERS VIE FOR CITY CHAMPIONSHIP

In their second year of varsity football, the North Shore Tigers have gained a shot at the city championship. Last Saturday in the play-offs, the Tigers defeated the Western High School Cowboys, <u>thus eliminated that team</u> from contention. Most of the credit for the
(1)
team's improvement must go to Joe Harris, the coach. <u>To play as well as they do</u> now,
(2)
the coach must have given the team superior instruction. There is no doubt that,

<u>if a coach is effective, his influence is over</u> many young minds.
(3)

With this major victory behind them, the Tigers can now look forward <u>to meet the</u>
(4)
defending champions, the Revere Minutemen, in the finals.

The win over the Cowboys was <u>due</u> to North Side's supremacy in the air. The Tigers'
(5)
players have the advantages of strength and of <u>being speedy</u>. Our sterling quarterback, Butch
(6)
Carter, a master of the long pass, used <u>these kind of passes</u> to bedevil the boys from Western.
(7)
As a matter of fact, if the Tigers <u>would have used</u> the passing offense earlier in the game, the
(8)
score would have been more one-sided. Butch, by the way, our all-around senior student, has already been tapped for bigger things. Having the highest marks in his class, <u>Barton College</u>

2 (#1)

has offered him a scholarship.
         (9)

The team's defense is another story. During the last few weeks, neither the linebackers nor the safety man <u>have shown</u> sufficient ability to contain their opponents' running game. In
                                                              (10)
the city final, <u>the defensive unit's failing to complete it's assignments</u> may lead to disaster.
                                        (11)
However, the coach said that this unit <u>not only has been cooperative but also the coach raise</u>
                                                                        (12)
<u>their eagerness to learn</u>. He also said that this team <u>has not and never will give up</u>. This kind
                                                                    (13)
of spirit is contagious, <u>therefore</u> I predict that the Tigers will win because I have <u>affection and full</u>
                              (14)   (15)
<u>confidence in</u> the team.

One of the happy surprises this season is Peter Yisko, our punter. Peter <u>is</u> in the United
                                                                                                   (16)
States for only two years. When he was in grammar school in the old country, it was not necessary for him <u>to have studied</u> hard. Now, he depends on the football team to help him with
                                        (17)
his English. Everybody <u>but the team mascot and I have</u> been pressed into service. Peter was
                                        (18
ineligible last year when he <u>learned that he would only obtain half</u> of the credits he had
                                              (19)
completed in Europe. Nevertheless, he attended occasional practice sessions, but he soon found out that, if one wants to be a successful player, <u>you</u> must realize that regular practice is
                                                                                      (20)
required. In fact, if a team is to be successful, it is necessary that everyone <u>be</u> present for all
                                                                                                       (21)
practice sessions. "The life of a football player," says Peter, "is better than <u>a scholar</u>."
                                                                                                      (22)

Facing the Minutemen, the Tigers will meet their most formidable opposition yet. This team <u>is not only gaining a bad reputation</u> but also indulging in illegal practices on the field.
         (23)
They <u>can't hardly object to us being</u> technical about penalties under these circumstances.
            (24)
As far as the Minutemen are concerned, a <u>victory will taste sweet like a victory should</u>.
                                                            (25)

1. A. that eliminated that team   B. and they were eliminated   1.____
    C. and eliminated them   D. Correct as is

3 (#1)

2. A. To make them play as well as they do
    B. Having played so well
    C. After they played so well
    D. Correct as is

2.____

3. A. if coaches are effective; they have influence over
    B. to be effective, a coach influences over
    C. if a coach is effective, he influences
    D. Correct as is

3.____

4. A. to meet with   B. to meeting
    C. to a meeting of   D. Correct as is

4.____

5. A. because of   B. on account of
    C. motivated by   D. Correct as is

5.____

6. A. operating swiftly   B. speed
    C. running speedily   D. Correct as is

6.____

7. A. these kinds of pass B. this kind of passes
    C. this kind of pass   D. Correct as is

7.____

8. A. would of used   B. had used
    C. were using   D. Correct as is

8.____

9. A. he was offered a scholarship by Barton College.
    B. Barton College offered a scholarship to him.
    C. a scholarship was offered him by Barton College
    D. Correct as is

9.____

10. A. had shown   B. were showing
    C. has shown   D. Correct as is

10.____

11. A. the defensive unit failing to complete its assignment
    B. the defensive unit's failing to complete its assignment
    C. the defensive unit failing to complete it's assignment
    D. Correct as is

11.____

12. A. has been not only cooperative, but also eager to learn
    B. has not only been cooperative, but also shows eagerness to learn
    C. has been not only cooperative, but also they were eager to learn
    D. Correct as is

12.____

13. A. has not given up and never will
    B. has not and never would give up
    C. has not given up and never will give up
    D. Correct as is

13.____

53

14. A. .Therefore B. : therefore 14.____
    C. —therefore D. Correct as is

15. A. full confidence and affection for 15.____
    B. affection for and full confidence in
    C. affection and full confidence concerning
    D. Correct as is

16. A. is living B. was living 16.____
    C. has been D. Correct as is

17. A. to study B. to be studying 17.____
    C. to have been studying D. Correct as is

18. A. but the team mascot and me has 18.____
    B. but the team mascot and myself has
    C. but the team mascot and me have
    D. Correct as is

19. A. only learned that he would obtain half 19.____
    B. learned that he would obtain only half
    C. learned that he only would obtain half
    D. Correct as is

20. A. a person B. one 20.____
    C. one D. every

21. A. is B. will be 21.____
    C. shall be D. Correct as is

22. A. to be a scholar B. being a scholar 22.____
    C. that of a scholar D. Correct as is

23. A. not only is gaining a bad reputation 23.____
    B. is gaining not only a bad reputation
    C. is not gaining only a bad reputation
    D. Correct as is

24. A. can hardly object to us being B. can hardly object to our being 24.____
    C. can't hardly object to our being D. Correct as is

25. A victory will taste sweet like it should 25.____
    B. victory will taste sweetly as it should taste
    C. victory will taste sweet as a victory should
    D. Correct as is

Questions 26-30.

DIRECTIONS: Questions 26 through 30 are to be answered on the basis of the instructions and paragraph which follow.

The paragraph which follows is part of report prepared by a buyer for submission to his superior. The paragraph contains 5 underlined groups of words, each one bearing a number which identifies the question relating to it. Each of these groups of words MAY or MAY NOT represent standard written English, suitable for use in a formal report. For each question, decide whether the group of words used in the paragraph which is always choice A is standard written English and should be retained, or whether choice B, C, or D.

On October 23, 2009 the vendor delivered two microscopes to the using agency. <u>When they inspected</u>, one microscope was found to have a defective part. The vendor was
(26)
notified, and offered to replace the defective part; the using agency, however, requested <u>that the microscope be replaced</u>. The vendor claimed that complete replacement was
(27)
unnecessary and refused to comply with the agency's demand, <u>having the result that the
(28)
agency declared</u> that it will pay only for the acceptable microscope. At that point <u>I got involved by the agency's contacting me</u>. The agency requested that I speak to the vendor
(29)
since I handled the original purchase and have dealed with this vendor before.
(30)

26. A. When they inspected
    B. Upon inspection
    C. The inspection report said that
    D. Having inspected,

27. A. that the microscope be replaced
    B. a whole new microscope in replacement
    C. to have a replacement for the microscope
    D. that they get the microscope replaced

28. A. , having the result that the agency declared
    B. ; the agency consequently declared
    C. , which refusal caused the agency to consequently declare
    D. , with the result of the agency's declaring

29. A. I got involved by the agency's contacting me
    B. I became involved, being contacted by the agency
    C. the agency contacting me, I got involved
    D. the agency contacted me and I became involved

30. A. have dealed with this vendor before.
    B. done business before with this vendor.
    C. know this vendor by prior dealings
    D. have dealt with this vendor before.

30._____

KEY (CORRECT ANSWERS)

1.	C	11.	B	21.	D
2.	A	12.	A	22.	C
3.	C	13.	B	23.	D
4.	B	14.	A	24.	A
5.	A	15.	B	25.	C
6.	B	16.	C	26.	B
7.	C	17.	A	27.	A
8.	B	18.	A	28.	B
9.	D	19.	B	29.	D
10.	C	20.	C	30.	D

SPELLING

EXAMINATION SECTION

TEST 1

DIRECTIONS: In each of the following tests in this part, select the letter of the one MISSPELLED word in each of the following groups of words. *PRINT THE LETTER OF THE CORRECT ANSWER IN THE SPACE AT THE RIGHT.*

1.	A. grateful	B. fundimental	C. census	D. analysis	1.____
2.	A. installment	B. retrieve	C. concede	D. dissapear	2.____
3.	A. accidentaly	B. dismissal	C. conscientious	D. indelible	3.____
4.	A. perceive	B. carreer	C. anticipate	D. acquire	4.____
5.	A. facillity	B. reimburse	C. assortment	D. guidance	5.____
6.	A. plentiful	B. across	C. advantagous	D. similar	6.____
7.	A. omission	B. pamphlet	C. guarrantee	D. repel	7.____
8.	A. maintenance	B. always	C. liable	D. anouncement	8.____
9.	A. exaggerate	B. sieze	C. condemn	D. commit	9.____
10.	A. pospone	B. altogether	C. grievance	D. excessive	10.____
11.	A. banana	B. trafic	C. spectacle	D. boundary	11.____
12.	A. commentator	B. abbreviation	C. battaries	D. monastery	12.____
13.	A. practically	B. advise	C. pursuade	D. laboratory	13.____
14.	A. fatigueing	B. invincible	C. strenuous	D. ceiling	14.____
15.	A. propeller	B. reverence	C. piecemeal	D. underneth	15.____
16.	A. annonymous	B. envelope	C. transit	D. variable	16.____
17.	A. petroleum	B. bigoted	C. meager	D. resistence	17.____

2 (#1)

18. A. permissible   B. indictment   C. fundemental   D. nowadays   18.____

19. A. thief   B. bargin   C. nuisance   D. vacant   19.____

20. A. technique   B. vengeance   C. aquatic   D. heighth   20.____

KEY (CORRECT ANSWERS)

1. B. fundamental
2. D. disappear
3. A. accidentally
4. B. career
5. A. facility

6. C. advantageous
7. C. guarantee
8. D. announcement
9. B. seize
10. A. postpone

11. B. traffic
12. C. batteries
13. C. persuade
14. A. fatiguing
15. D. underneath

16. A. anonymous
17. D. resistance
18. C. fundamental
19. B. bargain
20. D. height

TEST 2

DIRECTIONS: In each of the following tests in this part, select the letter of the one MISSPELLED word in each of the following groups of words. *PRINT THE LETTER OF THE CORRECT ANSWER IN THE SPACE AT THE RIGHT.*

1. A. apparent B. superintendent C. relieve D. calendar 1.____
2. A. foreign B. negotiate C. typical D. disipline 2.____
3. A. posponed B. argument C. susceptible D. deficit 3.____
4. A. preferred B. column C. peculiar D. equiped 4.____
5. A. exaggerate B. disatisfied C. repetition D. already 5.____
6. A. livelihood B. physician C. obsticle D. strategy 6.____
7. A. courageous B. ommission C. ridiculous D. awkward 7.____
8. A. sincerely B. abundance C. negligable D. elementary 8.____
9. A. obsolete B. mischievous C. enumerate D. atheletic 9.____
10. A. fiscel B. beneficiary C. concede D. translate 10.____
11. A. segregate B. excessivly C. territory D. obstacle 11.____
12. A. unnecessary B. monopolys C. harmonious D. privilege 12.____
13. A. sinthetic B. intellectual C. gracious D. archaic 13.____
14. A. beneficial B. fulfill C. sarcastic D. disolve 14.____
15. A. umbrella B. sentimental C. inefficent D. psychiatrist 15.____
16. A. noticable B. knapsack C. librarian D. meant 16.____
17. A. conference B. upheaval C. vulger D. odor 17.____
18. A. surmount B. pentagon C. calorie D. inumerable 18.____
19. A. classifiable B. moisturize C. monitor D. assesment 19.____
20. A. thermastat B. corrupting C. approach D. thinness 20.____

KEY (CORRECT ANSWERS)

1. C. relieve
2. D. discipline
3. A. postponed
4. D. equipped
5. B. dissatisfied

6. C. obstacle
7. B. omission
8. C. negligible
9. D. athletic
10. A. fiscal

11. B. excessively
12. B. monopolies
13. A. synthetic
14. D. dissolve
15. C. inefficient

16. A. noticeable
17. C. vulgar
18. D. innumerable
19. D. assessment
20. A. thermostat

TEST 3

DIRECTIONS: In each of the following tests in this part, select the letter of the one MISSPELLED word in each of the following groups of words. *PRINT THE LETTER OF THE CORRECT ANSWER IN THE SPACE AT THE RIGHT.*

1. A. typical   B. descend   C. summarize   D. continuel   1.____
2. A. courageous   B. recomend   C. omission   D. eliminate   2.____
3. A. compliment   B. illuminate   C. auxilary   D. installation   3.____
4. A. preliminary B. aquainted   C. syllable   D. analysis   4.____
5. A. accustomed   B. negligible   C. interupted   D. bulletin   5.____
6. A. summoned   B. managment   C. mechanism   D. sequence   6.____
7. A. commitee   B. surprise   C. noticeable   D. emphasize   7.____
8. A. occurrance   B. likely   C. accumulate   D. grievance   8.____
9. A. obstacle   B. particuliar   C. baggage   D. fascinating   9.____
10. A. innumerable B. seize   C. applicant   D. dictionery   10.____
11. A. monkeys   B. rigid   C. unnatural   D. roomate   11.____
12. A. surveying   B. figurative   C. famous   D. curiosety   12.____
13. A. rodeo   B. inconcievable C. calendar   D. magnificence   13.____
14. A. handicaped B. glacier   C. defiance   D. emperor   14.____
15. A. schedule   B. scrawl   C. seclusion   D. sissors   15.____
16. A. tissues   B. tomatos   C. tyrants   D. tragedies   16.____
17. A. casette   B. graceful   C. penicillin   D. probably   17.____
18. A. gnawed   B. microphone   C. clinicle   D. batch   18.____
19. A. amateur   B. altitude   C. laborer   D. expence   19.____
20. A. mandate   B. flexable   C. despise   D. verify   20.____

KEY (CORRECT ANSWERS)

1. D. continual
2. B. recommend
3. C. auxiliary
4. B. acquainted
5. C. interrupted

6. B. management
7. A. committee
8. A. occurrence
9. B. particular
10. D. dictionary

11. D. roommate
12. D. curiosity
13. B. inconceivable
14. A. handicapped
15. D. scissors

16. B. tomatoes
17. A. cassette
18. C. clinical
19. D. expense
20. B. flexible

TEST 4

DIRECTIONS: In each of the following tests in this part, select the letter of the one MISSPELLED word in each of the following groups of words. *PRINT THE LETTER OF THE CORRECT ANSWER IN THE SPACE AT THE RIGHT.*

1. A. primery   B. mechanic   C. referred   D. admissible   1.____
2. A. cessation   B. beleif   C. aggressive   D. allowance   2.____
3. A. leisure   B. authentic   C. familiar   D. contemtable   3.____
4. A. volume   B. forty   C. dilemma   D. seldum   4.____
5. A. discrepancy B. aquisition   C. exorbitant   D. lenient   5.____
6. A. simultanous B. penetrate   C. revision   D. conspicuous   6.____
7. A. ilegible   B. gracious   C. profitable   D. obedience   7.____
8. A. manufacturer B. authorize   C. compelling   D. pecular   8.____
9. A. anxious   B. rehearsal   C. handicaped   D. tendency   9.____
10. A. meticulous   B. accompaning   C. initiative   D. shelves   10.____
11. A. hammaring   B. insecticide   C. capacity   D. illogical   11.____
12. A. budget   B. luminous   C. aviation   D. lunchon   12.____
13. A. moniter   B. bachelor   C. pleasurable   D. omitted   13.____
14. A. monstrous   B. transistor   C. narrative   D. anziety   14.____
15. A. engagement   B. judical   C. pasteurize   D. tried   15.____
16. A. fundimental B. innovation   C. perpendicular D. extravagant   16.____
17. A. bookkeeper   B. brutality   C. gymnaseum   D. cemetery   17.____
18. A. sturdily   B. pretentious   C. gourmet   D. enterance   18.____
19. A. resturant   B. tyranny   C. kindergarten   D. ancestry   19.____
20. A. benefit   B. possess   C. speciman   D. noticing   20.____

KEY (CORRECT ANSWERS)

1. A. primary
2. B. belief
3. D. contemptible
4. D. seldom
5. B. acquisition

6. A. simultaneous
7. A. illegible
8. D. peculiar
9. C. handicapped
10. B. accompanying

11. A. hammering
12. D. luncheon
13. A. monitor
14. D. anxiety
15. B. judicial

16. A. fundamental
17. C. gymnasium
18. D. entrance
19. A. restaurant
20. C. specimen

———

TEST 5

DIRECTIONS: In each of the following tests in this part, select the letter of the one MISSPELLED word in each of the following groups of words. *PRINT THE LETTER OF THE CORRECT ANSWER IN THE SPACE AT THE RIGHT.*

1. A. arguing   B. correspondance   1.____
    C. forfeit   D. dissension
2. A. occasion   B. description   C. prejudice   D. elegible   2.____
3. A. accomodate   B. initiative   C. changeable   D. enroll   3.____
4. A. temporary   B. insistent   C. benificial   D. separate   4.____
5. A. achieve   B. dissappoint   C. unanimous   D. judgment   5.____
6. A. procede   B. publicly   C. sincerity   D. successful   6.____
7. A. deceive   B. goverment   C. preferable   D. repetitive   7.____
8. A. emphasis   B. skillful   C. advisible   D. optimistic   8.____
9. A. tendency   B. rescind   C. crucial   D. noticable   9.____
10. A. privelege   B. abbreviate   C. simplify   D. divisible   10.____
11. A. irresistible   B. varius   C. mutual   D. refrigerator   11.____
12. A. amateur   B. distinguish   C. rehearsal   D. poision   12.____
13. A. biased   B. ommission   C. precious   D. coordinate   13.____
14. A. calculated   B. enthusiasm   C. sincerely   D. parashute   14.____
15. A. sentry   B. materials   C. incredable   D. budget   15.____
16. A. chocolate   B. instrument   C. volcanoe   D. shoulder   16.____
17. A. ancestry   B. obscure   C. intention   D. ninty   17.____
18. A. artical   B. bracelet   C. beggar   D. hopeful   18.____
19. A. tournament   B. sponsor   C. perpendiclar   D. dissolve   19.____
20. A. yeild   B. physician   C. greasiest   D. admitting   20.____

KEY (CORRECT ANSWERS)

1. B. correspondence
2. D. eligible
3. A. accommodate
4. C. beneficial
5. B. disappoint

6. A. proceed
7. B. government
8. C. advisable
9. D. noticeable
10. A. privilege

11. B. various
12. D. poison
13. B. omission
14. D. parachute
15. C. incredible

16. C. volcano
17. D. ninety
18. A. article
19. C. perpendicular
20. A. yield

TEST 6

DIRECTIONS: In each of the following tests in this part, select the letter of the one MISSPELLED word in each of the following groups of words. *PRINT THE LETTER OF THE CORRECT ANSWER IN THE SPACE AT THE RIGHT.*

1. A. achievment   B. maintenance   C. questionnaire   D. all are correct   1._____
2. A. prevelant   B. pronunciation C. separate   D. all are correct   2._____
3. A. permissible   B. relevant   C. seize   D. all are correct   3._____
4. A. corroborate   B. desparate   C. eighth   D. all are correct   4._____
5. A. exceed   B. feasibility   C. psycological   D. all are correct   5._____
6. A. parallel   B. aluminum   C. calendar   D. eigty   6._____
7. A. microbe   B. ancient   C. autograph   D. existance   7._____
8. A. plentiful   B. skillful   C. amoung   D. capsule   8._____
9. A. erupt   B. quanity   C. opinion   D. competent   9._____
10. A. excitement   B. discipline   C. luncheon   D. regreting   10._____
11. A. magazine   B. expository   C. imitation   D. permenent   11._____
12. A. ferosious   B. machinery   C. precise   D. magnificent   12._____
13. A. conceive   B. narritive   C. separation   D. management   13._____
14. A. muscular   B. witholding   C. pickle   D. glacier   14._____
15. A. vehicel   B. mismanage   C. correspondence   D. dissatisfy   15._____
16. A. sentince   B. bulletin   C. notice   D. definition   16._____
17. A. appointment   B. exactly   C. typest   D. light   17._____
18. A. penalty   B. suparvise   C. consider   D. division   18._____
19. A. schedule   B. accurate   C. corect   D. simple   19._____
20. A. suggestion   B. installed   C. proper   D. agincy   20._____

KEY (CORRECT ANSWERS)

1. A. achievement
2. B. prevalent
3. D. all are correct
4. B. desperate
5. C. psychological

6. D. eighty
7. D. existence
8. C. among
9. B. quantity
10. D. regretting

11. D. permanent
12. A. ferocious
13. B. narrative
14. B. withholding
15. A. vehicle

16. A. sentence
17. C. typist
18. B. supervise
19. C. correct
20. D. agency

TEST 7

DIRECTIONS: In each of the following tests in this part, select the letter of the one MISSPELLED word in each of the following groups of words. *PRINT THE LETTER OF THE CORRECT ANSWER IN THE SPACE AT THE RIGHT.*

1. A. symtom   B. serum   B. antiseptic   D. aromatic   1._____
2. A. register   B. registrar   C. purser   D. burser   2._____
3. A. athletic   B. tragedy   C. batallion   D. sophomore   3._____
4. A. latent   B. godess   C. aisle   D. whose   4._____
5. A. rhyme   B. rhythm   C. thime   D. thine   5._____
6. A. eighth   B. exaggerate   C. electoral   D. villain   6._____
7. A. statute   B. superintendent   7._____
   C. iresistible   D. colleague
8. A. sieze   B. therefor   C. auxiliary   D. changeable   8._____
9. A. siege   B. knowledge   C. lieutenent   D. weird   9._____
10. A. acquitted   B. polititian   C. professor   D. conqueror   10._____
11. A. changeable   B. chargeable   C. salable   D. useable   11._____
12. A. promissory   B. prisoner   C. excellent   D. tyrany   12._____
13. A. conspicuous B. essance   C. comparative   D. brilliant   13._____
14. A. notefying   B. accentuate   C. adhesive   D. primarily   14._____
15. A. exercise   B. sublime   C. stuborn   D. shameful   15._____
16. A. presume   B. transcript   C. strech   D. wizard   16._____
17. A. specify   B. regional   C. arbitrary   D. segragation   17._____
18. A. requirement B. happiness   C. achievement   D. gently   18._____
19. A. endurance   B. fusion   C. balloon   D. enormus   19._____
20. A. luckily   B. schedule   C. simplicity   D. sanwich   20._____

KEY (CORRECT ANSWERS)

1. A. symptom
2. D. bursar
3. C. battalion
4. B. goddess
5. C. thyme

6. C. electoral
7. C. irresistible
8. A. seize
9. C. lieutenant
10. B. politician

11. D. usable
12. D. tyranny
13. B. essence
14. A. notifying
15. C. stubborn

16. C. stretch
17. D. segregation
18. D. gently
19. D. enormous
20. D. sandwich

TEST 8

DIRECTIONS: In each of the following tests in this part, select the letter of the one MISSPELLED word in each of the following groups of words. *PRINT THE LETTER OF THE CORRECT ANSWER IN THE SPACE AT THE RIGHT.*

1. A. maintain   B. maintainance   C. sustain   D. sustenance   1.____
2. A. portend   B. portentious   C. pretend   D. pretentious   2.____
3. A. prophesize   B. prophesies   C. farinaceous   D. spaceous   3.____
4. A. choose   B. chose   C. choosen   D. chasten   4.____
5. A. censure   B. censorious   C. pleasure   D. pleasurable   5.____
6. A. cover   B. coverage   C. adder   D. adage   6.____
7. A. balloon   B. diregible   C. direct   D. descent   7.____
8. A. whemsy   B. crazy   C. flimsy   D. lazy   8.____
9. A. derision   B. pretention   C. sustention   D. contention   9.____
10. A. question   B. questionaire   C. legion   D. legionary   10.____
11. A. chattle   B. cattle   C. dismantle   D. kindle   11.____
12. A. canal   B. cannel   C. chanel   D. colonel   12.____
13. A. hemorrage   B. storage   C. manage   D. foliage   13.____
14. A. surgeon   B. sturgeon   C. luncheon   D. stancheon   14.____
15. A. diploma   B. commission   C. dependent   D. luminious   15.____
16. A. likelihood   B. blizzard   C. machanical   D. suppress   16.____
17. A. commercial   B. releif   C. disposal   D. endeavor   17.____
18. A. operate   B. bronco   C. excaping   D. grammar   18.____
19. A. orchard   B. collar   C. embarass   D. distant   19.____
20. A. sincerly   B. possessive   C. weighed   D. waist   20.____

KEY (CORRECT ANSWERS)

1. B. maintenance
2. B. portentous
3. D. spacious
4. C. chosen
5. D. pleasurable

6. D. adage
7. B. dirigible
8. A. whimsy
9. B. pretension
10. B. questionnaire

11. A. chattel
12. C. channel
13. A. hemorrhage
14. D. stanchion
15. D. luminous

16. C. mechanical
17. B. relief
18. C. escaping
19. C. embarrass
20. A. sincerely

———

TEST 9

DIRECTIONS: In each of the following tests in this part, select the letter of the one MISSPELLED word in each of the following groups of words. *PRINT THE LETTER OF THE CORRECT ANSWER IN THE SPACE AT THE RIGHT.*

1. A. statute   B. stationary   C. staturesque   D. stature   1.____
2. A. practicible   B. practical   C. particle   D. reticule   2.____
3. A. plague   B. plaque   C. ague   D. aigrete   3.____
4. A. theology   B. idealogy   C. psychology   D. philology   4.____
5. A. dilema   B. stamina   C. feminine   D. strychnine   5.____
6. A. deceit   B. benefit   C. grieve   D. hienous   6.____
7. A. commensurable B. measurable   C. duteable   D. salable   7.____
8. A. homogeneous   B. heterogeneous   8.____
   C. advantageous   D. religeous
9. A. criticize   B. dramatise   C. exorcise   D. exercise   9.____
10. A. ridiculous   B. comparable   C. merciful   D. cotten   10.____
11. A. antebiotic   B. stitches   C. pitiful   D. sneaky   11.____
12. A. amendment   B. candadate   12.____
    C. accountable   D. recommendation
13. A. avocado   B. recruit   C. tripping   D. probally   13.____
14. A. calendar   B. desirable   C. familar   D. vacuum   14.____
15. A. deteriorate   B. elligible   C. liable   D. missile   15.____
16. A. amateur   B. competent   C. mischeivous   D. occasion   16.____
17. A. friendliness B. saleries   C. cruelty   D. ammunition   17.____
18. A. wholesome   B. cieling   C. stupidity   D. eligible   18.____
19. A. comptroller   B. traveled   C. accede   D. procede   19.____
20. A. Britain   B. Brittainica   C. conductor   D. vendor   20.____

KEY (CORRECT ANSWERS)

1. C. statuesque
2. A. practicable
3. D. aigrette
4. B. ideology
5. A. dilemma

6. D. heinous
7. C. dutiable
8. D. religious
9. B. dramatize
10. D. cotton

11. A. antibiotic
12. B. candidate
13. D. probably
14. C. familiar
15. B. eligible

16. C. mischievous
17. B. salaries
18. B. ceiling
19. D. proceed
20. B. Brittanica

———

TEST 10

DIRECTIONS: In each of the following tests in this part, select the letter of the one MISSPELLED word in each of the following groups of words. *PRINT THE LETTER OF THE CORRECT ANSWER IN THE SPACE AT THE RIGHT.*

1. A. lengthen   B. region   C. gases   D. inspecter   1.____
2. A. imediately   B. forbidden   2.____
   C. complimentary   D. aeronautics
3. A. continuous   B. paralel   C. opposite   D. definite   3.____
4. A. Antarctic   B. Wednesday   C. Febuary   D. Hungary   4.____
5. A. transmission   B. exposure   C. pistol   D. customery   5.____
6. A. juvinile   B. martyr   C. deceive   D. collaborate   6.____
7. A. unnecessary   B. repetitive   C. cancellation   D. airey   7.____
8. A. transit   B. availible   C. objection   D. galaxy   8.____
9. A. ineffective   B. believeable   C. arrangement   D. aggravate   9.____
10. A. possession   B. progress   C. reception   D. predjudice   10.____
11. A. congradulate   B. percolate   C. major   D. leisure   11.____
12. A. convenience   B. privilige   C. emerge   D. immerse   12.____
13. A. erasable   B. inflammable   C. audable   D. laudable   13.____
14. A. final   B. fines   C. finis   D. Finish   14.____
15. A. emitted   B. representative   15.____
    C. discipline   D. insistance
16. A. diphthong   B. rarified   C. library   D. recommend   16.____
17. A. compel   B. belligerent   C. successful   D. sergeant   17.____
18. A. dispatch   B. dispise   C. dispose   D. dispute   18.____
19. A. administrator   B. adviser   C. diner   D celluler   19.____
20. A. ignite   B. ignision   C. igneous   D. ignited   20.____

75

KEY (CORRECT ANSWERS)

1.	D. inspector		11.	A. congratulate
2.	A. immediately		12.	B. privilege
3.	B. parallel		13.	C. audible
4.	C. February		14.	D. Finnish
5.	D. customary		15.	D. insistence
6.	A. juvenile		16.	B. rarefied
7.	D. airy		17.	D. sergeant
8.	B. available		18.	B. despise
9.	B. believable		19.	D. cellular
10.	D. prejudice		20.	B. ignition

TEST 11

DIRECTIONS: In each of the following tests in this part, select the letter of the one MISSPELLED word in each of the following groups of words. *PRINT THE LETTER OF THE CORRECT ANSWER IN THE SPACE AT THE RIGHT.*

1. A. repellent B. secession C. sebaceous D. saxaphone 1._____
2. A. navel B. counteresolution 2._____
   C. marginalia D. perceptible
3. A. Hammerskjold B. Nehru C. U Thamt D. Krushchev 3._____
4. A. perculate B. periwinkle C. perigee D. retrogression 4._____
5. A. buccaneer B. tobacco C. buffalo D. oscilate 5._____
6. A. siege B. wierd C. seize D. cemetery 6._____
7. A. equaled B. bigoted C. benefited D. kaleideoscope 7._____
8. A. blamable B. bullrush C. questionnaire D. irascible 8._____
9. A. tobogganed B. acquiline C. capillary D. cretonne 9._____
10. A. daguerrotype B. elegiacal C. iridescent D. inchoate 10._____
11. A. bayonet B. braggadocio C. corollary D. connoiseur 11._____
12. A. equinoctial B. fusillade C. fricassee D. potpouri 12._____
13. A. octameter B. impressario C. hyetology D. hieroglyphics 13._____
14. A. innanity B. idyllic C. fylfot D. inimical 14._____
15. A. liquefy B. rarefy C. putrify D. sapphire 15._____
16. A. canonical B. stupified C. millennium D. memorabilia 16._____
17. A. paraphenalia B. odyssey 17._____
    C. onomatopoeia D. osseous
18. A. peregrinate B. pecadillo C. reptilian D. uxorious 18._____
19. A. pharisaical B. vicissitude C. puissance D. wainright 19._____
20. A. holocaust B. tesselate C. scintilla D. staccato 20._____

KEY (CORRECT ANSWERS)

1. D. saxophone
2. B. counterresolution
3. C. U Thant
4. A. percolate
5. D. oscillate

6. B. weird
7. D. kaleidoscope
8. B. bulrush
9. B. aquiline
10. A. daguerreotype

11. D. connoisseur
12. D. potpourri
13. B. impresario
14. A. inanity
15. C. putrefy

16. B. stupefied
17. A. paraphernalia
18. B. peccadillo
19. D. wainwright
20. B. tessellate

———

TEST 12

DIRECTIONS: In each of the following tests in this part, select the letter of the one MISSPELLED word in each of the following groups of words. *PRINT THE LETTER OF THE CORRECT ANSWER IN THE SPACE AT THE RIGHT.*

1. A. questionnaire B. gondoleer C. chandelier D. acquiescence 1.____
2. A. surveilance B. surfeit C. vaccinate D. belligerent 2.____
3. A. occassionally B. recurrence C. silhouette D. incessant 3.____
4. A. transferral B. benefical C. descendant D. dependent 4.____
5. A. separately B. flouresence C. deterrent D. parallel 5.____
6. A. acquittal B. enforceable C. counterfeit D. indispensible 6.____
7. A. susceptible B. accelarate C. exhilarate D. accommodation 7.____
8. A. impedimenta B. collateral C. liason D. epistolary 8.____
9. A. inveigle B. panegyric C. reservoir D. manuver 9.____
10. A. synopsis B. paraphernalia C. affidavit D. subpoena 10.____
11. A. grosgrain B. vermilion C. abbatoir D. connoiseur 11.____
12. A. gabardine B. camoflage C. hemorrhage D. contraband 12.____
13. A. opprobrious B. defalcate C. fiduciery D. recommendations 13.____
14. A. nebulous B. necessitate C. impricate D. discrepancy 14.____
15. A. discrete B. condescension C. condign D. condiment 15.____
16. A. cavalier B. effigy C. legitimatly D. misalliance 16.____
17. A. rheumatism B. vaporous C. cannister D. hallucinations 17.____
18. A. paleonthology B. octogenarian C. gradient D. impingement 18.____
19. A. fusilade B. fusilage C. ensilage D. desiccate 19.____
20. A. rationale B. raspberry C. reprobate D. varigated 20.____

KEY (CORRECT ANSWERS)

1. B. gondolier
2. A. surveillance
3. A. occasionally
4. B. beneficial
5. B. fluorescence

6. D. indispensable
7. B. accelerate
8. C. liaison
9. D. maneuver
10. B. paraphernalia

11. D. connoisseur
12. B. camouflage
13. C. fiduciary
14. C. imprecate
15. B. condescension

16. C. legitimately
17. C. canister
18. A. paleontology
19. A. fusillade
20. D. variegated

READING COMPREHENSION
UNDERSTANDING WRITTEN MATERIALS
COMMENTARY

The ability to read and understand written materials—texts, publications, newspapers, orders, directions, expositions—is a skill basic to a functioning democracy and to an efficient business or viable government.

That is why almost all examinations—for beginning, middle, and senior levels—test reading comprehension, directly or indirectly.

The reading test measures how well you understand what you read. This is how it is done: You read a passage followed by several statements. From these statements, you choose the one statement, or answer, that is BEST supported by, or BEST matches, what is said in the paragraph. PRINT THE LETTER OF THE CORRECT ANSWER IN THE SPACE AT THE RIGHT.

SAMPLE QUESTION

DIRECTIONS: Answer Question 1 ONLY according to the information given in the following passage.

1. A cashier has to make many arithmetic calculations in connection with his work. Skill in arithmetic comes readily with practice; no special talent is needed.
On the basis of the above statement, it is MOST accurate to state that
   A. the most important part of a cashier's job is to make calculations
   B. few cashiers have the special ability needed to handle arithmetic problems easily
   C. without special talent, cashiers cannot learn to do the calculations they are required to do in their work
   D. a cashier can, with practice, learn to handle the computations he is required to make

1.____

The CORRECT answer is D.

EXAMINATION SECTION
TEST 1

DIRECTIONS: Questions 1 through 5 are to be answered on the basis of the following reading passage. *PRINT THE LETTER OF THE CORRECT ANSWER IN THE SPACE AT THE RIGHT.*

The size of each collection route will be determined by the amount of waste per stop, distance between stops, speed of loading, speed of truck, traffic conditions during loading time, etc.

Basically, the route should consist of a proper amount of work for a crew for the daily work period. The crew should service all properties eligible for this service in their area. Routes should, whenever practical, be compact, with a logical progression through the area. Unnecessary travel should be avoided. Traffic conditions on the route should be thoroughly studied to prevent lost time in loading, to reduce hazards to employees, and to minimize tying up of regular traffic movements by collection forces. Natural and physical barriers and arterial streets should be used as route boundaries wherever possible to avoid lost time in travel.

Routes within a district should be laid out so that the crews start at the point farthest from the disposal area and, as the day progresses, move toward that area, thus reducing the length of the haul. When possible, the work of the crews in a district should be parallel as they progress throughout the day, with routes finishing up within a short distance of each other. This enables the supervisor to be present when crews are completing their work and enables him to shift crews to trouble spots to complete the day's work.

1. Based on the above passage, an advantage of having collection routes end near one another is that
    A. routes can be made more compact
    B. unnecessary travel is avoided, saving manpower
    C. the length of the haul is reduced
    D. the supervisor can exercise better manpower control

1.____

2. Of the factors mentioned above which affect the size of a collection route, the two over which the sanitation forces have LEAST control are
    A. amount of waste; traffic conditions
    B. speed of loading; amount of waste
    C. speed of truck; distance between stops
    D. traffic conditions; speed of truck

2.____

3. According to the above passage, the size of a collection route is probably good if
    A. it is a fair day's work for a normal crew
    B. it is not necessary for the trucks to travel too fast
    C. the amount of waste collected can be handled properly
    D. the distance between stops is approximately equal

3.____

4. Based on the above passage, it is reasonable to assume that a sanitation officer laying out collection routes should NOT try to have
   A. an arterial street as a route boundary
   B. any routes near the disposal area
   C. the routes overlap a little
   D. the routes run in the same direction

5. The term "logical progression," as used in the second paragraph of the passage refers MOST NEARLY to
   A. collecting from street after street in order
   B. numbering streets one after the other
   C. rotating crew assignments
   D. using logic as a basis for assigned crews

KEY (CORRECT ANSWERS)

1. D
2. A
3. A
4. C
5. A

TEST 2

DIRECTIONS: Questions 1 through 3 are to be answered on the basis of the following reading passage. *PRINT THE LETTER OF THE CORRECT ANSWER IN THE SPACE AT THE RIGHT.*

    In an open discussion designed to arrive at solutions to community problems, the person leading the discussion group should give the members a chance to make their suggestions before he makes his. He must not be afraid of silence; if he talks just to keep things going, he will find he can't stop, and good discussion will not develop. In other words, the more he talks, the more the group will depend on him. If he finds, however, that no one seems ready to begin the discussion, his best "opening" is to ask for definitions of terms which form the basis of the discussion. By pulling out as many definitions or interpretations as possible, he can get the group started "thinking out load," which is essential to good discussion.

1. According to the above passage, good group discussion is MOST likely to result if the person leading the discussion group
    A. keeps the discussion going by speaking whenever the group stops speaking
    B. encourages the group to depend on him by speaking more than any other group member
    C. makes his own suggestions before the group has a chance to make theirs
    D. encourages discussion by asking the group to interpret the terms to be discussed

1.____

2. According to the above passage, "thinking out loud" by the discussion group is
    A. *good* practice, because "thinking out loud" is important to good discussion
    B. *poor* practice, because group members should think out their ideas before discussing them
    C. *good* practice, because it will encourage the person leading the discussion to speak more
    D. *poor* practice, because it causes the group to fear silence during discussion

2.____

3. According to the above passage, the one of the following which is LEAST desirable at an open discussion is having
    A. silent periods during which none of the group members speaks
    B. differences of opinion among the group members concerning the definition of terms
    C. a discussion leader who uses "openings" to get the discussion started
    D. a discussion leader who provides all suggestions and definitions for the group

3.____

KEY (CORRECT ANSWERS)

1. D
2. A
3. D

TEST 3

DIRECTIONS: Questions 1 through 4 are to be answered on the basis of the following reading passage. *PRINT THE LETTER OF THE CORRECT ANSWER IN THE SPACE AT THE RIGHT.*

The insects you will control are just a minute fraction of the millions which inhabit the world. Man does well to hold his own in the face of the constant pressures that insects continue to exert upon him. Not only are the total numbers tremendous, but the number of individual kinds, or species, certainly exceeds 800,000—number greater than that of all other animals combined. Many of these are beneficial but some are especially competitive with man. Not only are insects numerous, but they are among the most adaptable of all animals. In their many forms, they are fitted for almost any specific way of life. Their adaptability, combined with their tremendous rate of reproduction, gives insects an unequaled potential for survival!

The food of insects includes almost anything that can be eaten by any other animal as well as many things which cannot even be digested by any other animals. Most insects do not harm the products of man or carry diseases harmful to him; however, many do carry diseases and others feed on his food and manufactured goods. Some are adapted to living only in open areas while others are able to live in extremely confined spaces. All of these factor combined make the insects a group of animals having many members which are a nuisance to man and thus of great importance.

The control of insects requires an understanding of their way of life. Thus, it is necessary to understand the anatomy of the insect, its method of growth, the time it takes for the insect to grow from egg to adult, its habits, the stage of its life history in which it causes damage, its food, and its common living places. In order to obtain the best control, it is especially important to be able to identify correctly the specific insect involved because, without this knowledge, it is impossible to prescribe a proper treatment.

1. Which one of the following is a CORRECT statement about the insect population of the world, according to the above passage? The
    A. total number of insects is less than the total number of all other animals combined
    B. number of species of insects is greater than the number of species of all other animals combined
    C. total number of harmful insects is less than the number of species of those which are harmful
    D. number of species of harmless insects is less than the number of species of those which are harmful

2. Insects will be controlled MOST efficiently if you
    A. understand why the insects are so numerous
    B. know what insects you are dealing with
    C. see if the insects compete with man
    D. are able to identify the food which the insects digest

3. According to the above passage, insects are of importance to a scientist PRIMARILY because they
   A. can be annoying, destructive, and harmful to man
   B. are able to thrive in very small spaces
   C. cause damage during their growth stages
   D. are so adaptable that they can adjust to any environment

4. According to the above passage, insects can eat
   A. everything that any other living thing can eat
   B. man's food and thing which he makes
   C. anything which other animals can't digest
   D. only food and food products

KEY (CORRECT ANSWERS)

1. B
2. B
3. A
4. B

TEST 4

DIRECTIONS: Questions 1 through 3 are to be answered on the basis of the following reading passage. *PRINT THE LETTER OF THE CORRECT ANSWER IN THE SPACE AT THE RIGHT.*

Telephone service in a government agency should be adequate and complete with respect to information given or action taken. It must be remembered that telephone contacts should receive special consideration since the caller cannot see the operator. People like to feel that they are receiving personal attention and that their requests or criticisms are receiving individual rather than routine consideration. All this contributes to what has come to be known as *tone of service*. The aim is to use standards which are clearly very good or superior. The factors to be considered in determining what makes good tone of service are speech, courtesy, understanding, and explanations. A caller's impression of tone of service will affect the general public attitude toward the agency and city services in general.

1. The above passage states that people who telephone a government agency like to feel that they are
   A. creating a positive image of themselves
   B. being given routine consideration
   C. receiving individual attention
   D. setting standards for telephone service

2. Which one of the following is NOT mentioned in the above passage as a factor in determining good tone of service?
   A. Courtesy   B. Education   C. Speech   D. Understanding

3. The above passage implies that failure to properly handle telephone calls is MOST likely to result in
   A. a poor impression of city agencies by the public
   B. a deterioration of courtesy toward operators
   C. an effort by operators to improve the Tone of Service
   D. special consideration by the public of operator difficulties

KEY (CORRECT ANSWERS)

1. C
2. B
3. A

TEST 5

DIRECTIONS: Questions 1 through 5 are to be answered on the basis of the following reading passage. *PRINT THE LETTER OF THE CORRECT ANSWER IN THE SPACE AT THE RIGHT.*

For some office workers it is useful to be familiar with the four main classes of domestic mail; for others, it is essential. Each class has a different rate of postage and some have requirements concerning wrapping, sealing, or special information to be placed on the package.

First-class mail, the class which may not be opened for postal inspection, includes letters, postcards, business reply cards, and other kinds of written matter. There are different rates for some of the kinds of cards which can be sent by first-class mail. The maximum weight for an item sent by first-class mail is 70 pounds. An item which is not letter size should be marked "First Class: on all sides.

Although office workers most often come into contact with first-class mail, they may find it helpful to know something about the other classes. Second-class mail is generally used for mailing newspapers and magazines. Publishers of these articles must meet certain U.S. Postal Service requirements in order to obtain a permit to use second-class mailing rates. Third-class mail, which must weigh less than 1 pound, includes printed materials and merchandise parcels. There are two rate structure for this class, a single-piece rate and a bulk rate. Fourth-class mail, also known as parcel post, includes packages weighing from one to 40 pounds. For more information about these classes of mail and the actual mailing rates, contact our local post office.

1. According to this passage, first-class mail is the only class which   1._____
   A. has a limit on the maximum weight of an item
   B. has different rates for items within the class
   C. may not be opened for postal inspection
   D. should be used by office workers

2. According to this passage, the one of the following items which may CORRECTLY   2._____
   be sent by fourth-class mail is a
   A. magazine weighing one-half pound
   B. package weighing one-half pound
   C. package weighing two pounds
   D. postcard

3. According to this passage, there are different postage rates for   3._____
   A. a newspaper sent by second-class mail and a magazine sent by second-class mail
   B. each of the classes of mail
   C. each pound of fourth-class mail
   D. printed material sent by third-class mail and merchandise parcels sent by third-class mail

4. In order to send a newspaper by second-class mail, a publisher must 4.____
   A. have met certain postal requirements and obtained a permit
   B. indicate whether he wants to use the single-piece or the bulk rate
   C. make certain that the newspaper weighs less than one pound
   D. mark the newspaper "Second Class" on the top and bottom of the wrapper

5. Of the following types of information, the one which is NOT mentioned in the passage is the 5.____
   A. class of mail to which parcel post belongs
   B. kinds of items which can be sent by each class of mail
   C. maximum weight for an item sent by fourth-class mail
   D. postage rate for each of the four classes of mail

KEY (CORRECT ANSWERS)

1. C
2. C
3. B
4. A
5. D

TEST 6

DIRECTIONS: Questions 1 through 5 are to be answered on the basis of the following reading passage. *PRINT THE LETTER OF THE CORRECT ANSWER IN THE SPACE AT THE RIGHT.*

The thickness of insulation necessary for the most economical results varies with the steam temperature. The standard covering consists of 85 percent magnesia with 10 percent of long-fibre asbestos as a binder. Both magnesia and laminated asbestos-felt and other forms of mineral wool including glass wool are also used for heat insulation. The magnesia and laminated-asbestos coverings may be safely used at temperatures up to 600°F. Pipe insulation is applied in molded sections 3 feet long; the sections are attached to the pipe by means of galvanized iron wire or netting. Flanges and fittings can be insulated by direct application of magnesia cement to the metal without *reinforcement*. Insulation should always be maintained inn good condition because it saves fuel. Routine maintenance of warm-pipe insulation should include prompt repair of damaged surfaces. Steam and hot-water leaks concealed by insulation will be difficult to detect. Underground steam or hot-water pipes are best insulated using a concrete trench with removable cover.

1. The word *reinforcement*, as used above, means MOST NEARLY   1.____
   A. resistance   B. strengthening
   C. regulation   D. removal

2. According to the above paragraph, magnesia and laminated asbestos   2.____
   coverings may be safely used at temperatures up to
   A. 800°F   B. 720°F   C. 675°F   D. 600°F

3. According to the above paragraph, insulation should *always* be maintained   3.____
   in good condition because it
   A. is laminated   B. saves fuel
   C. is attached to the pipe   D. prevents leaks

4. According to the above paragraph, pipe insulation sections are attached to the   4.____
   pipe by means of
   A. binders   B. mineral wool
   C. netting   D. staples

5. According to the above paragraph, a leak in a hot-water pipe may be difficult   5.____
   to detect because, when insulation is used, the leak is
   A. underground   B. hidden   C. routine   D. cemented

KEY (CORRECT ANSWERS)

1. B
2. D
3. B
4. C
5. B

TEST 7

DIRECTIONS: Questions 1 through 4 are to be answered on the basis of the following reading passage. *PRINT THE LETTER OF THE CORRECT ANSWER IN THE SPACE AT THE RIGHT.*

    Cylindrical surfaces are the most common form of finished surfaces found on machine parts, although flat surfaces are also very common; hence, many metal-cutting processes are for the purpose of producing either cylindrical or flat surfaces. The machines used for cylindrical or flat shapes may be, and often are, utilized also for forming the various irregular or special shapes required on many machine parts. Because of the prevalence of cylindrical and flat surfaces, the student of manufacturing practice should learn first about the machines and methods employed to produce these surfaces. The cylindrical surfaces may be internal as in holes and cylinders. Any one part may, of course, have cylindrical sections of different diameters and lengths and include flat ends or shoulders and, frequently, there is a threaded part or, possibly, some finished surface that is not circular in cross-section. The prevalence of cylindrical surfaces on machine parts explains why lathes are found in all machine shops. It is important to understand the various uses of the lathes because many of the operations are the same fundamentally as those performed on other types of machine tools.

1. According to the above passage, the MOST common form of finished surfaces found on machine parts is
   A. cylindrical   B. elliptical   C. flat   D. square

2. According to the above passage, any one part of cylindrical surfaces may have
   A. chases   B. shoulders   C. keyways   D. splines

3. According to the above passage, lathes are found in all machine shops because cylindrical surfaces on machine parts are
   A. scarce   B. internal   C. common   D. external

4. As used in the above paragraph, the word *processes* means
   A. operations   B. purposes   C. devices   D. tools

KEY (CORRECT ANSWERS)

1. A
2. B
3. C
4. A

TEST 8

DIRECTIONS: Questions 1 and 2 are to be answered on the basis of the following reading passage. *PRINT THE LETTER OF THE CORRECT ANSWER IN THE SPACE AT THE RIGHT.*

The principle of interchangeability requires manufacture to such specification that component parts of a device may be selected at random and assembled to fit and operate satisfactorily. Interchangeable manufacture, therefore, requires that parts be made to definite limits of error, and to fit gages instead of mating parts. Interchangeability does not necessarily involve a high degree of precision; stove lids, for example, are interchangeable but are not particularly accurate, and carriage bolts and nuts are not precision products but are completely interchangeable. Interchangeability may be employed in unit-production as well as mass-production systems of manufacture.

1. According to the above paragraph, in order for parts to be interchangeable, they must be
    A. precision-machined
    B. selectively-assembled
    C. mass-produced
    D. made to fit gages

    1.____

2. According to the above paragraph, carriage bolts are interchangeable because they are
    A. precision-made
    B. sized to specific tolerances
    C. individually matched products
    D. produced in small units

    2.____

KEY (CORRECT ANSWERS)

1. D
2. B

ARITHMETICAL REASONING
EXAMINATION SECTION
TEST 1

DIRECTIONS: Each question or incomplete statement is followed by several suggested answers or completions. Select the one that BEST answers the question or completes the statement. *PRINT THE LETTER OF THE CORRECT ANSWER IN THE SPACE AT THE RIGHT.*

1. In 2015, a public agency spent $180 to buy pencils that cost three cents each. In 2017, the agency spent $420 to buy the same number of pencils that it had bought in 2015.
   The price per pencil that the agency paid in 2017 was _____ cents.
   A. $6 1/3$ B. $2/3$ C. 7   D. $7 3/4$

   1._____

2. A stenographer spent her 35 hour work week on taking dictation, transcribing the dictate material, and filing.
   If she spent 20% of the work week on taking dictation and ½ of the remaining time on transcribing the dictated material, the number of hours of the work week that she spent on filing was
   A. 7   B. 10.5   C. 14   D. 17.4

   2._____

3. A typist typed eight pages in two hours.
   If she typed an average of 50 lines per page and an average of 12 words per line, what was her typing speed, in words per minute?
   A. 40   B. 50   C. 60   D. 80

   3._____

4. The daily compensation to be paid to each consultant hired in a certain agency is computed by dividing his professional earnings in the previous year by 250. The maximum daily compensation they can receive is $200 each. Four consultants who were hired to work on a special project had the following professional earnings in the previous year: $37,500, $144,000, $46,500, and $61,100.
   What will be the TOTAL daily cost to the agency for these four consultants?
   A. $932   B. $824   C. $736   D. $712

   4._____

5. In a typing and stenographic pool consisting of 30 employees, 2/5 of them are typists, 1/3 of them are senior typists and senior stenographers, and the rest are stenographers.
   If there are 5 more stenographers than senior stenographers, how many senior stenographers are in the typing and stenographic pool?
   A. 3   B. 5   C. 8   D. 10

   5._____

6. There are 3,330 copies of a three-page report to be collated. One clerk starts   6.____
   collating at 9:00 A.M. and is joined 15 minutes later by two other clerks. It
   takes 15 minutes for each of these clerks to collate 90 copies of the report.
   At what time should the job be completed if all three clerks continue working at
   the same rate without breaks?
   A. 12:00 Noon   B. 12:15 P.M.   C. 1:00 P.M.   D. 1:15 P.M.

7. By the end of last year, membership in the blood credit program in a certain   7.____
   agency had increased from the year before by 500, bringing the total to 2,500.
   If the membership increased by the same percentage this year, the TOTAL
   number of members in the blood credit program for this agency by the end of
   this year should be
   A. 2,625   B. 3,000   C. 3,125   D. 3,250

8. During this year, an agency suggestion program put into practice suggestions   8.____
   from 24 employee, thereby saving the agency 40 times the amount of money it
   paid in awards.
   If $1/3$ of the employees were awarded $50 each, ½ of the employees were
   awarded $25 each, and the rest were awarded $10 each, how much money did
   the agency save by using the suggestions?
   A. $18,760   B. $29,600   C. $32,400   D. $46,740

9. A senior stenographer earned $20,100 a year and had 4.5% state tax withheld   9.____
   for the year.
   If she was paid every two weeks, the amount of state tax that was taken out of
   each of her paychecks, based on a 52-week year, was MOST NEARLY
   A. $31.38   B. $32.49   C. $34.77   D. $36.99

10. Two stenographers have been assigned to address 750 envelopes. One   10.____
    stenographer addresses twice as many envelopes per hour as the other
    stenographer.
    If it takes five hours for them to complete the job, the rate of the slower
    stenographer is _____ envelopes per hour.
    A. 35   B. 50   C. 75   D. 100

11. Suppose that the postage rate for mailing single copies of a magazine to   11.____
    persons not included on a subscription list is 18 cents for the first two ounces of
    the single copy and 3 cents for each additional ounce.
    Of 19 copies of a magazine, each of which weighs eleven ounces, are mailed
    to 19 different people, the TOTAL postage cost of these magazines is
    A. $3.42   B. $3.99   C. $6.18   D. $8.55

12. A senior stenographer spends about 40 hours a month taking dictation. Of   12.____
    that time, 44% is spent taking minutes of meetings, 38% if spent taking
    dictation of lengthy reports, and the rest of the time is spent taking dictation of
    letters and memoranda.
    How much more time is spent taking minutes of meetings than n taking
    dictation of letters and memoranda? 10 hours _____ minutes.
    A. 6   B. 16   C. 24   D. 40

3 (#1)

13. In one week, a stenographer typed 65 letter. Forty letters had 4 copies on colored paper. The rest had 3 copies on colored paper.
    If the stenographer had 50 sheets of colored paper on hand at the beginning of the week when she started typing the letters, how many sheets of colored paper did she have left at the end of the week?
    A. 190   B. 235   C. 265   D. 305

    13._____

14. An agency is planning to microfilm letters and other correspondence of the last five years. The number of letter-size documents that can be photographed on a 100-foot roll of microfilm is 2,995. The agency estimates that it will need 240 feet of microfilm to do all the pages of all of the letters.
    How many pages of letter-size documents can be photographed on this microfilm?
    A. 5,990   B. 6,785   C. 7,188   D. 7,985

    14._____

15. In an agency, $2/3$ of the total number of female stenographers and ½ of the total number of male stenographers attended a general staff meeting.
    If there are a total of 56 stenographers in the agency and 25% of them are male, the number of female stenographers who attended the general staff meeting is
    A. 14   B. 28   C. 36   D. 42

    15._____

16. A worker is currently earning $17,140 a year and pays $350 a month for rent. He expects to get a raise that will enable him to move into an apartment where his rent will be 25% of his new yearly salary.
    If this new apartment is going to cost him $390 a month, what is the TOTAL amount of raise that he expects to get?
    A. $480   B. $980   C. $1,580   D. $1,840

    16._____

17. The tops of five desks in an office are to be covered with a scratch-resistant material. Each desk top measures 60 inches by 36 inches.
    How many square feet of material will be needed for the five desk tops?
    A. 15   B. 75   C. 96   D. 180

    17._____

18. Three grades of bond paper are used in a central transcribing unit. The cost per ream of paper is $1.90 for Grade A, $1.70 for Grade B, and $1.60 for Grade C.
    If the central transcribing unit used 6 reams of Grade A paper, 14 reams of Grade B paper, and 20 reams of Grade C paper, the AVERAGE cost, per ream, of the bond paper used by this unit is between
    A. $1.62 and $1.66   B. $1.66 and $1.70
    C. $1.70 and $1.74   D. $1.73 and $1.80

    18._____

19. The Complaint Bureau of a city agency is composed of an investigation unit, a clerical unit, and a central transcribing unit. The sum of $264,000 has been appropriated for the operation of this bureau. Of this sum, $170,000 is to be allotted to the clerical unit.

    19._____

4 (#1)

Of this bureau's total appropriation, the percentage that is left for the central transcribing unit is MOST NEARLY _____ if 41,200 is allotted for investigations.
   A. 20%   B. 30%   C. 40%   D. 50%

20. Three typists were assigned to address a total of 2,655 postcards. Typist A addressed postcards at the rate of 170 per hour. Typist B addressed the postcards at the rate of 150 per hour. Typist C's rate is not known. After the three typists had addressed postcards for three and a half hours, Typist C was taken off this assignment. It was necessary for Typist A and Typist B to work two and a half hours more to complete this assignment. The rate per hour at which Typist C addressed the postcards was
   A. less than 150
   B. between 150 and 170
   C. more than 170 but less than 200
   D. more than 200

20.____

21. In 2015, a city agency bought 12,000 envelopes at $4.00 per hundred. In 2016, the price of envelopes purchased was 40 percent higher than the 2010 price, but only 60 percent as many envelopes were bought.
The total cost of the envelopes purchased in 2016 was MOST NEARLY
   A. $250   B. $320   C. $400   D. $480

21.____

22. A stenographer has been assigned to place entries on 500 forms. She places entries on 25 forms by the end of half an hour, when she is joined by another stenographer. The second stenographer places entries at the rate of 45 an hour.
Assuming both stenographers continue to work at their respective rates of speed, the TOTAL number of hours required to carry out the entire assignment is
   A. 5   B. 5½   C. 6½   D. 7

22.____

23. On Monday, a stenographer took dictation without interruption for 1½ hours and transcribed all the dictated material in 3½ hours. On Tuesday, she took dictation uninterruptedly for 1¾ hours and transcribed all the material in 3¾ hours. On Wednesday, she took dictation without interruption for 2¼ hours and transcribed all the material in 4½ hours.
If she took dictation at the average rate of 90 words per minute during these three days, then her average transcription rate, in words per minute, for the same three days was MOST NEARLY
   A. 36   B. 41   C. 54   D. 58

23.____

24. In a division of clerks and stenographers, 15 people are currently employed, 20% of whom are stenographers.
If management plans are to maintain the current number of stenographers, but to increase the clerical staff to the point where 12% of the total staff are stenographers, what is the MAXIMUM number of additional clerks that should be hired to meet these plans?
   A. 3   B. 8   C. 10   D. 12

24.____

5 (#1)

25. In the first quarter of the year, a certain operator sent out 230 quarterly reports. 25._____
In the second quarter of that year, he sent out 310 quarterly reports.
The percent increase in the number of quarterly reports he sent out in the
second quarter of the year compared to the first quarter of the year is MOST
NEARLY
    A. 26%   B. 29%   C. 35%   D. 39%

KEY (CORRECT ANSWERS)

1.	C	11.	D
2.	C	12.	C
3.	A	13.	C
4.	C	14.	C
5.	A	15.	B
6.	B	16.	C
7.	C	17.	B
8.	B	18.	B
9.	C	19.	A
10.	B	20.	D

21.	C
22.	B
23.	B
24.	C
25.	C

6 (#1)

SOLUTIONS TO PROBLEMS

1. $180 ÷ .03 = 6000 pencils bought. In 2017, the price per pencil = $420/6000 = .07 = 7 cents

2. Number of hours on filing = 35 − (.20)(35) · (½)(28) = 14

3. Eight pages contain (8)(50)(12) = 4800 words. She thus typed 4800 words in 120 minutes = 40 words per minute

4. $37,500 ÷ 250 = $150; $144,000 ÷ 250 = $576; $46,500 ÷ 250 = $186; $61,100 ÷ 250 = $244.40. Since $200 = maximum compensation for any single consultant, total compensation = $150 + $200 + $186 + $200 = $736

5. Number of typists = (2/5)(30) = 12, number of senior typists and senior stenographers = ($1/3$)(30) = 10, number of stenographers = 30 − 12 − 10 = 8. Finally, number of senior stenographers = 8 − 5 = 3

6. At 9:15 A.M., 90 copies have been collated. The remaining 3,240 copies are being collated at the rate of (3)(90) = 270 every 15 minutes = 1080 per hour. Since 3240 ÷ 1080 = 3 hours, the clerks will finish at 9:15 A.M. + 3 hours = 12:15 P.M.

7. During the last year, the membership increased from 2000 to 2500, which represents a (500/2000)(100) = 25% increase. A 25% increase during this year means the membership = (2500)(1.25) = 3125

8. Total awards = ($1/3$)(24)($50) + (½)(24)($25) + ($1/6$)(24)($10) = $740. Thus, the savings = (40)($740) = $29,600

9. Her pay for 2 weeks = $20,100 ÷ 26 ≈ $773.08. Thus, her state tax for 2 weeks = ($773.08)(.045) ≈ $34.79. (Nearest correct answer is $34.77 in four selections.)

10. 750 ÷ 5 hours = 150 envelopes per hour for the 2 stenographers combined. Let x = number of envelopes addressed by the slower stenographer. Then, x + 2x = 150. Solving, = 50

11. Total cost = (19)[.18+(.03)(9)] = $8.55

12. (.44)(40) − (.18)(40) = 10.4 hours = 10 hrs. 24 min.

13. 500 − (40)(4) − (25)(3) = 265

14. 2995 ÷ 100 = 29.95 documents per foot of microfilm roll. Then, (29.95)(240 ft) = 7188 documents

15. There are (.75)(56) = 42 female stenographers. Then, ($2/3$)(42) = 28 of them attended the meeting

7 (#1)

16. ($390)(12) = $4679 new rent per year. Then, ($4680)(4) = $18,720 = his new yearly salary. His raise = $18,720 - $17,140 = $1580

17. Number of sq. ft. = (5)(60)(36) ÷ 144 = 75

18. Average cost per ream = [(1.90)(6) + ($1.70)(14) + ($1.60)(20)] /40 = $1.68, which is between $1.66 and $1.77

19. $264,000 - $170,000 - $41,200 = 52,800 = 20%

20. Let x = typist C's rate. Since Typists A and B each worked 6 hrs., while Typist C worked only 3.5 hours, we have (6)(170) + (6)(150) + 3.5x = 2655. Solving, x = 210, which is mre than 200

21. In 2016, the cost per hundred envelopes was ($4.00)(1.40) = $5.60 and (.60)(12,000) = 7200 envelopes were bought. Total cost in 2016 = (72)($5.60) = $403.20, or about $400

22. The first stenographer's rate is 50 forms per hour. After ½ hour, there are 500 – 25 = 475 forms to be done and the combined rate of the 2 stenographers is 95 forms per hr. Thus, total hours required = ½ + (475) ÷ (95) = 5½

23. Total time for dictation = 1¼ + 1¾ + 2¼ = 5¼ hrs. = 315 min. The number of words = (90)(315) = 28,350. The total transcription 3 time = 3¼ + 3¾ + 44 = 11½ hrs. = 690 min. Her average transcription rate = 28,350 ÷ 690 ≈ 41 words per min.

24. Currently, there are (.20)(15) = 3 stenographers, and thus 12 clerks. Let x = additional clerks. Then, $\frac{3}{3+12+x}$ = .12. This simplifies to 3 = (.12)(15+x). Solving, x = 10

25. Percent increase = $(\frac{80}{230})(100)$ ≈ 35%

TEST 2

DIRECTIONS: Each question or incomplete statement is followed by several suggested answers or completions. Select the one that BEST answers the question or completes the statement. *PRINT THE LETTER OF THE CORRECT ANSWER IN THE SPACE AT THE RIGHT.*

1. A school has 112 homeroom classes. There were 15 school days in February. The aggregate register of the school for the month of February was 52,920; the aggregate attendance was 43,860.
   The average class size, to the NEAREST tenth, is
      A. 35.3   B. 31.5   C. 29.2   D. 26.9

   1.____

2. As the school secretary in charge of supplies, you are asked to order the following items on a supplementary requisition for general supplies:
   - 5 gross of red pencils at $8.90 per dozen
   - 5,000 manila envelopes at $2.35 per C
   - 36 rulers at $187.20 per gross
   - 6 boxes of manila paper at $307.20 per carton (24 boxes to a carton)
   - 180 reams of composition paper at $27.80 per carton (20 reams to a carton)

   The TOTAL amount of the order is
      A. $957.20   B. $1,025.30   C. $916.80   D. $991.30

   2.____

3. In the high school to which you have been assigned as a school secretary, the annual allotment for general supplies, textbooks, repairs, etc. for the school year 2015-16 was $37,500. A special allotment of $10,000 was granted for textbooks ordered from the State Textbook List. The original requisition for general and vocational supplies amounted to $12,514.75; for science supplies, $6,287.75; for textbooks, including the special funds, $13,785.00; monies spent for equipment repairs and science perishables through December 31, 2015, $1,389.68.
   The balance in your supply allotment account on January 1, 2016 will be
      A. $14,913.00 B. $13,523.32 C. $17,308.32 D. $3,523.32

   3.____

4. The teacher of one of the sixth term typing classes in the high school to which you are assigned as a school secretary has agreed to have her students type attendance cards for the incoming students for the new schoolyear, commencing in September, as a work project. There are 24 students in the class; each student can complete 8 cards during a typing period. There will be 4,032 new students in September.
   The number of typing periods required to complete the task is
      A. 31   B. 21   C. 28   D. 24

   4.____

5. As a school secretary assigned to payroll duties, you are required to prepare the extra-curricular payroll report for the coaches teams in your high school. The rate of pay for these activities was increased on November 1 from $148 per session to $174.50 per session. The pay period which you are reporting is for the months of October, November, and December. Mr. Jones, the football coach, conducted 15 practice sessions in October, 20 in November, and 30 in December.

   5.____

102

2 (#2)

His TOTAL gross pay on the December extra-curricular payroll report is
A. $10,547.50   B. $10,415.00   C. $10,945.00   D. $11,342.50

6. The comparative results on a uniform examination given in your school for the last three years follow:

	2014	2015	2016
Number Taking Test	501	496	485
Number Passing Test	441	437	436

The percentage of passing, to the nearest tenth of a percent, for the year in which the HIGHEST percent of students passed is
A. 89.3%   B. 88%   C. 89.9%   D. 90.3%

6._____

7. During his first seven terms in high school, a student compiled the following averages:

Term	Numbers of Majors Completed	Average
1	4	81.25%
2	4	83.75%
3	5	86.2%
4	5	85.8%
5	5	87.0%
6	5	83.4%
7	5	82.6%

In his eighth term, the student had the following final marks in major subjects: 90%, 95%, 80%, 90%, 85%. The student's average for all eight terms of high school, correct to the nearest tenth of a percent, is
A. 84.8%   B. 84.7%   C. 84.9%   D. 85.8%

7._____

8. A secretary is asked by her employer to order an office machine which lists at a price of $360, less trade discounts of 20% and 10%, terms 2/10, n/30. There is a delivery charge of $8 and an installation charge of $12.
If the machine is paid for in 10 days, the TOTAL cost of the machine will be
A. $264.80   B. $258.40   C. $266.96   D. $274.02

8._____

9. The school to which you have been assigned as school secretary has an annual allowance of 5,120 hours for all teacher aides. The principal decides to employ 5 teacher aides from 8:00 A.M. to 12:00 Noon, and 5 other teacher aides from 12:00 Noon to 4:00 P.M. daily for as many days as his allowance permits.
If a teacher aide earns $17.00 an hour, and he is present every day, his TOTAL earnings for the school year will be more than
A. $7,000 but less than $8,000   B. $8,000 but less than $9,000
C. $9,000 but less than $10,000   D. $10,000

9._____

10. During examination week in a high school to which you have been assigned as school secretary, teachers are required to be in school at least 6 hours and 20 minutes daily although their arrival and departure times may vary each day. A teacher's time card that you have been asked to check shows the following entries for the week of June 17:

Date	Arrival	Departure
17	7:56 A.M.	2:18 P.M.
18	9:54 A.M.	4:22 P.M.
19	12:54 P.M.	7:03 P.M.
20	9:51 A.M.	4:15 P.M.
21	7:58 A.M.	2:11 P.M.

During the week of June 17 to June 21, the teacher was in school for AT LEAST the minimum required time on _____ days.
  A. 2 of the 5   B. 3 of the 5   C. 4 of the 5   D. all 5

10.____

11. As school secretary, you are asked to find the total of the following bill received in your school:
    750 yellow envelopes at $.22 per C
    2,400 white envelopes at $2.80 per M
    30 rulers at $5.04 per gross
The TOTAL of the bill is
  A. $69.90   B $24.27   C. $18.87   D. $9.42

11.____

12. A department in the school to which you have been assigned as school secretary has been given a textbook allowance of $5,50 for the school year. The department's textbook order is:
    75 books at $32.50 each
    45 books at $49.50 each
    25 books at $34.50 each
The TOTAL of the department's order is _____ the allowance.
  A. $27.50 over   B. $27.50 under
  C. $72.50 under   D. $57.50 over

12.____

13. The total receipts, including 5% city sales tax, for the G.O. store for the first week of school amounted to $489.09.
The receipts from the G.O. store for the first week of school, excluding the 5% city sales tax, amounted to
  A. $465.89   B. $364.64   C. $464.63   D. $513.54

13.____

14. Class sizes in the school to which you have been assigned as school secretary are as follows:

Number of Classes	Class Size
9	29
12	31
15	32
7	33
11	34

14.____

The average class size in this school, correct to the nearest tenth, is
A. 30.8 B. 31.9 C. 31.8 D. 30.9

15. In 2013, the social security tax was 4.2% for the first $6,600 earned a year. In 2014, the social security tax was 4.4% on the first $6,600 earned a year. For a teacher aide earning $19,200 in 2013 and $20,400 in 2014, the increase in social security tax deduction in 2014 over 2013 was
A. $132.00 B. $13.20 C. $19.20 D. $20.40

16. A teacher aide earning $23,900 a year will incur automatic deductions of 3.90% for social security and .50% for Medicare, based on the first $6,600 a year earnings.
The TOTAL deduction for these two items will be
A. $274 B. $290.40 C. $525.80 D. $300.40

17. The school store turns in receipts totaling $131.25 to the school treasurer, including 5% which has been collected for sales tax.
The amount of money which the treasurer MUST set aside for sales tax is
A. $6.56 B. $6.25 C. $5.00 D. $5.25

18. One of the custodial assistants can wash all the windows in the main office in 3 hours. A second assistant can wash the windows in the main office in 2 hours.
If the two men work together, they should complete the task in _____ hour(s) _____ minutes.
A. 1; 0 B. 1.5; 0 C. 1; 12 D. 1; 15

19. A school secretary is requested by the principal to order an office machine which lists at a price of $120, less discounts of 10% and 5%.
The net price of the machine to the school will be
A. $100.50 B. $102.00 C. $102.60 D. $103.00

20. Five students are employed at school under a work-study program through which they are paid $10.00 an hour for work in school offices, but no student may earn more than $450 a month. Three days before the end of the month, you note that the student payroll totals $2,062.50.
The number of hours which each of the students may work during the remainder of the month is _____ hour(s).
A. 4 B. 2 C. 1 D. 3

21. You are asked to summarize expenditures made by the school within the budget allocation for the school year. You determine that the following expenditures have been made: educational supplies, $2,600; postage, $650; emergency repairs, $225; textbooks, $5,100; instructional equipment, $1,200. Since $10,680 has been allocated to the school, the following sum still remains available for office supplies.
A. $905 B. $1,005 C. $800 D. $755

5 (#2)

22. In preparing the percentage of attendance for the period report, you note that the aggregate attendance is 57,585 and the aggregate register is 62,000. The percentage of attendance, to the nearest tenth of a percent, is
   A. 91.9%   B. 93.0%   C. 92.8%   D. 92.9%

22.____

23. You borrow $1,200 from your retirement fund which you must repay over a period of three years, with interest of $144, each payment to be divided equally among 36 total payments.
The monthly deduction from your paycheck will be
   A. $37.33   B. $36.00   C. $33.00   D. $37.30

23.____

24. Tickets for a school dance are printed, starting with number 401 and ending with number 1650. They are to be sold for $7.50 each. The tickets remaining unsold should start with number 1569.
The amount of cash which should be collected for the sale of tickets is
   A. $876.75   B. $937.50   C. $876.00   D. $875.25

24.____

25. Stage curtains are purchased by the school and delivered on October 3 under terms of 5/10, 2/30, net/60. The curtains are paid in full by a check for $522.50 on October 12.
The invoice price was
   A. $533.16   B. $522.50   C. $540.00   D. $550.00

25.____

KEY (CORRECT ANSWERS)

1.	B	11.	D
2.	B	12.	A
3.	B	13.	A
4.	B	14.	C
5.	C	15.	B
6.	C	16.	B
7.	C	17.	B
8.	D	18.	C
9.	B	19.	C
10.	B	20.	D

21. A
22. D
23. A
24. C
25. D

6 (#2)

SOLUTIONS TO PROBLEMS

1. Average class size = 52,920 ÷ 15 ÷ 112 = 31.5

2. Total amount = (5)(12)($8.90) + (50)($2.35) + (36)($187.20) ÷ 144 + (6)($307.20) ÷ 24 + (9)($27.80) = $1,025.30

3. Balance = $37,500 + $10,000 - $12,514.75 - $6,287.25 - $13,785 - $1,389.68 = $13,523.32

4. (24)(8) = 192 cards completed in one period. Then, 4032 ÷ 192 = 21 typing periods required

5. Total pay = (15)($148.00) + (20)($174.50) + (30)($174.50) = $10,945.00

6. The passing rates for 2014, 2015, and 2016 were 88.0%, 88.1%, and 89.9%, respectively. So, 89.9% was the highest

7. His 8th term average was 88.0%. His overall average for all 8 terms = [(4)(81.25%) + (4)(83.75%) + (5)(86.2%) + (5)(85.8%) + (5)(87.0%) + (5)(83.4%) + (5)(82.6%) + (5)(88.0%)] ÷ 38 = 84.9%

8. Total cost = ($360)(.80)(.90)(.98) + $8 + $12 ≈ $274.02 (Exact amount = $274.016)

9. 5120 ÷ 4 = 1280 teacher-days. Then, 1280 ÷ 20 = 128 days per teacher. A teacher's earnings for these 128 days = ($17.00)(4)(128) = $8,704, which is more than $8,000 but less than $9,000

10. The number of hours present on each of the 5 days listed was 6 hrs. 22 min., 6 hrs. 29 min., 6 hrs. 9 min., 6 hrs. 24 min., and 6 hrs. 13 min. On 3 days, he met the minimum time.

11. Total cost = (7.5)(.22) + (2.4)($2.80) + (30/144)(5.04) = $9.42

12. Textbook order = (75)($32.50) + (45)($49.50) + (25)($34.50) = $5,527.5, which is $27.50 over the allowance

13. Receipts without the tax = $489.09 ÷ 1.05 = $465.80

14. Average class size = [(9)(29) + (12)(31) + (7)(33) + (15)(32)] ÷ 54 ≈ 31.8

15. ($6,600)(.044-.042) = $13.20

16. ($6,600)(.039+.005) = $290.40

17. $131.25 = 1.05x, x = 125, $131.25 − 125.00 = 6.25

18. Let x = hours needed working together. Then, $(1/3)(x) + (1/2)(x) = 1$
    Simplifying, $2x + 3x = 6$. Solving, $x = 1\tfrac{1}{5}$ hrs. = 1 hr. 12 min.

19. Net price = 120 – 10% (12) = 108; 108 – 5% (5.40) = 102.60

20. ($225)(5) - $1031.25 = $93.75 remaining in the month. Since the 5 students earn $25 per hour combined, $93.75 ÷ $25 = 3.75, which must be rounded down to 3 hours

21. $10,680 - $2,600 - $650 - $225 - $5,100 - $1,200 = $905 for office supplies

22. 57,585 ÷ 62,000 ≈ .9288 ≈ 92.9%

23. Monthly deduction = $1344 ÷ 36 = $37.33. (Technically, 35 payments of $37.33 and 1 payment of $37.45)

24. (1569-401) = $876.00

25. The invoice price (which reflects the 5% discount) is $522.50 ÷ .95 = $550.00

TEST 3

DIRECTIONS: Each question or incomplete statement is followed by several suggested answers or completions. Select the one that BEST answers the question or completes the statement. *PRINT THE LETTER OF THE CORRECT ANSWER IN THE SPACE AT THE RIGHT.*

1. If an inch on an office layout drawing equals 4 feet of actual floor dimension, then a room which actually measures 9 feet by 14 feet is represented on the drawing by measurements equaling _____ inches × _____ inches.   1._____
   A. 2¼; 3½   B. 2½; 3½   C. 2¼; 3¼   D. 2½; 3¼

2. A cooperative education intern works from 1:30 P.M. to 5 P.M. on Mondays, Wednesdays, and Fridays, and from 10 A.M. to 2:30 P.M. with no lunch hour on Tuesdays and Thursdays. He earns $13.50 an hour on this job. In addition, he has a Saturday job paying $16.00 an hour at which he works from 9 A.M. to 3 P.M. with a half hour off for lunch.
   The gross amount that the student earns each week is MOST NEARLY   2._____
   A. $321.90   B. $355.62   C. $364.02   D. $396.30

3. Thirty-five percent of the College Discovery students who entered community college earned an associate degree. Of these students, 89% entered senior college, of which 67% went on to earn baccalaureate degrees.
   If there were 529 College Discovery students who entered community college, then the number of those who went on to finally receive a baccalaureate degree is MOST NEARLY   3._____
   A. 354   B. 315   C. 124   D. 110

4. It takes 5 office assistants two days to type 125 letters. Each of the assistants works at an equal rate of speed.
   How many days will it take 10 office assistants to type 200 letters?   4._____
   A. 1   B. 1³⁄₅   C. 2   D. 2¹⁄₅

5. The following are the grades and credits earned by Student X during the first two years in college.   5._____

Grade	Credits	Weight	Quality Points
A	10 ½	×4	
B	24	×3	
C	12	×2	
D	4 ½	×1	
F, FW	5	×0	

   To compute an index number:
   I. Multiply the number of credits of each grade by the weight to get the number of quality points
   II. Add the credits
   III. Add the quality points
   IV. Divide the total quality point by the total credits and carry the division to two decimal places

On the basis of the given information, the index number for Student X is
A. 2.55   B. 2.59   C. 2.63   D. 2.68

6. Typist X can type 20 forms per hour, and Typist Y can type 30 forms per hour. If there are 30 forms to be typed and both typists are put to work on the job, how son should they be expected to finish the work?
_____ minutes.
A. 32   B. 34   C. 36   D. 38

7. Assume that there were 18 working days in February and that the six clerks in your unit had the following number of absences:

Clerk	Absences
F	3
G	2
H	8
I	1
J	0
K	5

The average percentage attendance for the six clerks in your unit in February was MOST NEARLY
A. 80%   B. 82%   C. 84%   D. 86%

8. A certain employee is paid at the rate of $7.50 per hour, with time and a half for overtime. Hours in excess of 40 hours a week count as overtime. During the past week, the employee put in 48 working hours.
The employee's gross wages for the week are MOST NEARLY
A. $330   B. $350   C. $370   D. $390

9. You are making a report on the number of inside and outside calls handled by a particular switchboard. Over a 15-day period, the total number of all inside and outside calls handled by the switchboard was 5,760. The average number of inside calls per day was 234. You cannot find one day's tally of outside calls, but the total number of outside calls for the other fourteen days was 2,065.
From this information, how many outside calls must have been reported on the missing tally?
A. 175   B. 185   C. 195   D. 205

10. A floor plan has been prepared for a new building, drawn to a scale of ¾ inch = 1 foot. A certain area is drawn 1 and ½ feet long and 6 inches wide on the floor plan.
What are the ACTUAL dimensions of this area in the new building?
_____ feet long and _____ feet wide
A. 21; 8   B. 24; 8   C. 27; 9   D. 30; 9

11. You are preparing a package of six books to mail to a professor who is on sabbatical. They weigh, respectively, 1 pound 11 ounces, 1 pound 6 ounces, 2 pounds 1 ounce, 2 pounds 2 ounces, 1 pound 7 ounces, and 1 pound 8 ounces. The packaging material weighs 6 ounces.
    The TOTAL weight of the package will be _____ pounds _____ ounces.
    A. 10; 3   B. 10; 9   C. 11; 5   D. 12; 5

    11._____

12. Part-time students are charged $70 per credit for courses at a particular college. In addition, they musts pay a $24.00 student activity fee if they take six credits or more and $14.00 lab fee for each laboratory course.
    If a person takes one 3-credit course and one 4-credit course and his 4-credit course is a laboratory course, the TOTAL cost to him will be
    A. $504   B. $528   C. $542   D. $552

    12._____

13. The graduating course of a certain community college consisted of 378 majors in secretarial science, 265 majors in engineering science, 57 majors in nursing, 513 majors in accounting, and 865 majors in liberal arts.
    The percent of students who major in liberal arts at this college was MOST NEARLY
    A. 24.0%   B. 41.6%   C. 52.3%   D. 71.6%

    13._____

14. Donald Smith earns $12.80 an hour for forty hours a week, with time and a half for all hours over forty. Last week, his total earnings amounted to $627.20.
    He worked _____ hours.
    A. 46   B. 47   C. 48   D. 49

    14._____

15. Mr. Jones desires to sell an article costing $28 at a gross profit of 30% of the selling price, and to allow a trade discount of 20% of the list price.
    The list price of the article should be
    A. $43.68   B. $45.50   C. $48.00   D. $50.00

    15._____

16. The gauge of an oil storage tank in an elementary school indicates 1/5 full. After a truck delivers 945 gallons of oil, the gauge indicates 4/5 full.
    The capacity of the tank is _____ gallons.
    A. 1,260   B. 1,575   C. 1,625   D. 1,890

    16._____

17. An invoice dated April 3, terms 3/10, 2/30, net/60, was paid in full with a check for $787.92 on May 1.
    The amount of the invoice was
    A. $772.16   B. $787.92   C. $804.00   D. $812.29

    17._____

18. Two pipes supply the water for the swimming pool at Blenheim High School. One pipe can fill the pool in 9 hours. The second pipe can fill the pool in 6 hours.
    If both pipes were opened simultaneously, the pool could be filled in _____ hours _____ minutes.
    A. 3; 36   B. 4; 30   C. 5; 15   D. 7; 30

    18._____

19. John's father spent $24,000, which was one-fourth of his savings. He bought a car with three-eighths of the remainder of his savings.
His bank balance now amounts to
   A. $30,000   B. $32,000   C. $45,000   D. $50,000

20. A clock that loses 4 minutes every 24 hours was set at 6 A.M. on October 1 What time was indicated by the clock when the CORRECT time was 12:00 Noon on October 6th?
   A. 11:36   B. 11:38   C. $11:39   D. 11:40

21. Unit S's production fluctuated substantially from one year to another. In 2009, Unit s's production was 100% greater than in 2008. In 2010, production decreased by 25% from 2009. In 2011, Unit S's production was 10% greater than in 2010.
On the basis of this information, it is CORRECT to conclude that Unit S's production in 2011 exceeded Unit S's production in 2008 by
   A. 65%   B. 85%   C. 95%   D. 135%

22. Agency X is moving into a new building. It has 1,500 employees presently on its staff and does not contemplate much variance from this level. The new building contains 100 available offices, each with a maximum capacity of 30 employees. It has been decided that only 2/3 of the maximum capacity of each office will be utilized.
The TOTAL number of office that will be occupied by Agency X is
   A. 30   B. 65   C. 75   D. 90

23. One typist completes a form letter every 5 minutes and another typist completes one every 6 minutes.
If the two typists start together, how many minutes later will they again start typing new letters simultaneously and how many letters will they have completed by that time?
   A. 11; 30   B. 12; 24   C. 24; 12   D. 30; 1

24. During one week, a machine operator produces 10 fewer pages per hour of work than he usually does.
If it ordinarily takes him six hours to produce a 300-page report, how many hour LONGER will that same 300-page report take him during the week when he produces more slowly?
   A. 1½   B. 1²/₃   C. 2   D. 2¾

25. A study reveals that Miss Brown files N cards in M hours, and Miss Smith files the same number of cards in T hours.
If the two employees work together, the number of hours it will take them to file N cards is
   A. $\dfrac{N}{\frac{N}{M}+\frac{N}{N}}$ B. $\dfrac{N}{T+M}+\dfrac{2N}{MT}$ C. $N(\dfrac{M}{N}+\dfrac{N}{T})$ D. $\dfrac{N}{NT+MN}$

KEY (CORRECT ANSWERS)

1. A
2. B
3. D
4. B
5. A

6. C
7. B
8. D
9. B
10. B

11. B
12. B
13. B
14. A
15. D

16. B
17. C
18. A
19. C
20. C

21. A
22. C
23. D
24. A
25. A

SOLUTIONS TO PROBLEMS

1. 9/4 = 2¼" and 14/4 = 3½"

2. Gross amount = (3)($6.75)(3.5) + (2)($6.75)(4.5) + ($8.00)(5.5) = $174.624, which is closest to selection B ($177.81)

3. $(529)(.35)(.89)(.67) \approx 110$

4. 10 worker-days are needed to type 125 letters, so (200)(10) ÷ 125 = 16 worker-days are needed to type 200 letters. Finally, 16 ÷ 10 workers = 1 3/5 days

5. Index number = [(14)(10½) + (3)(24) + (2)(12) + (1)(4½) + (0)(5)] ÷ 56 ≈ 2,54

6. Typist X could do 30 forms in 30/20 = 1½ hours. Let x = number of hour needed when working together with Typist Y.
   Then, $(\frac{1}{1\frac{1}{2}})(x) + (\frac{1}{1})x = 1$. Simplifying, 2x + 3x = 3, so x = $\frac{3}{5}$ hr. = 36 min.

7. (3+2+8+1+0+5) ÷ 6 = 3.1$\overline{6}$. Then, 18 − 3.$\overline{6}$ = 14.8$\overline{3}$.

   Finally, 14.8$\overline{3}$ ÷ 18 ≈ 82%

8. Wages = ($7.50)(40) + ($11.25)(8) = $390

9. (234)(15) = 3510 inside calls. Then, 5760 − 3510 = 2259 outside calls. Finally, 2250 − 2065 = 185 outside calls on the missing day.

10. 18 ÷ ¾ - 24 feet long and 6 ÷ ¾ = 8 feet wide

11. Total weight = 1 lb. 11 oz. + 1 lb. 6 oz. + 2 lbs. 1 oz. + 2 lbs. 2 oz. + 1 lb. 7 oz. + 1 lb. 8 oz. + 6 oz = 8 lbs. 41 oz. 10 lbs. 9 oz.

12. Total cost = ($70)(7) + $24 + $14 = $528

13. 865 ÷ 2078 ≈ 41.6% liberal arts majors

14. ($12.80)(40) = $512, so he made $627.20 - $512 = $115.20 in overtime. His overtime rate = ($12.80)(1.5) = $19.20 per hour. Thus, he worked $115.20 ÷ $19.20 = 6 overtime hours. Total hours worked = 46

15. Let x = list price. Selling price = .80x. Then, .80x − (.30)(.80x) = $28. Simplifying, .56x = $28. Solving, x = $50.00

7 (#3)

16. 945 gallons represents $\frac{4}{5} \cdot \frac{1}{5} = \frac{3}{5}$ of the tank's capacity.

    Then, the capacity = $945 \div \frac{3}{5}$ = 1575 gallons

17. $787.92 ÷ .98 = $804.00

18. Let x = number of required hours. Then, (1/9)(x) + (1/6)(x) = 1
    Simplifying, 2x + 3x = 18. Solving, x = 3.6 hours = 3 hours 36 minutes

19. Bank balance = $96,000 - $24,000 – (3/8)($72,000) = $45,000

20. From Oct. 1, 6 A.M. to Oct. 6, Noon = 5½ days. The clock would show a loss of
    (4 min.)(5½) = 21 min. Thus, the clock's time would incorrectly) show 12:00 Noon – 21
    min. = 11:39 A.M.

21. 2008 = x, 2009 = 200x, 2010 = 150x, 2011 = 165x
    65% more

22. (2/3)(30) = 20 employees in each office. Then, 1500 ÷ 20 = 75 offices

23. After 30 minutes, the typists will have finished a total of 6 + 5 = 11 letters

24. When he works more slowly, he will only produce 300 – (6)(10) = 240 pages in 6 hrs.
    His new slower rate is 40 pages per hour, so he will need 60/40 = 1½ more hours to do
    the remaining 60 pages.

25. Let x = required hours. Then $(\frac{1}{M})(x) + (\frac{1}{10})(x) = 1$.

    Simplifying, x(T+M) = MT. Solving, x = MT/(T+M)

    Note: The N value is immaterial. Also, choice A reduces to MT/(T+M)

CLERICAL ABILITIES TEST
EXAMINATION SECTION
TEST 1

DIRECTIONS: Each question or incomplete statement is followed by several suggested answers or completions. Select the one that BEST answers the question or completes the statement. *PRINT THE LETTER OF THE CORRECT ANSWER IN THE SPACE AT THE RIGHT.*

Questions 1-10.

DIRECTIONS: Questions 1 through 10 consist of lines of names, dates, and numbers. For each question, you are to choose the option (A, B, C, or D) in Column II which EXACTLY matches the information in Column I. *PRINT THE LETTER OF THE CORRECT ANSWER IN THE SPACE AT THE RIGHT.*

SAMPLE QUESTION

Column I
Schneider 11/16/75 581932

Column II
A. Schneider 11/16/75 518932
B. Schneider 11/16/75 581932
C. Schnieder 11/16/75 581932
D. Shnieder 11/16/75 518932

The correct answer is B. Only Option B shows the name, date, and number exactly as they are in Column I. Option A has a mistake in the number. Option C has a mistake in the name. Option D has a mistake in the name and in the number. Now answer Questions 1 through 10 in the same manner.

Column I
1. Johnston 12/26/74 659251

Column II
A. Johnson 12/23/74 659251
B. Johston 12/26/74 659251
C. Johnston 12/26/74 695251
D. Johnston 12/26/74 659251

1.____

2. Allison 1/26/75 9939256

A. Allison 1/26/75 9939256
B. Alisson 1/26/75 9939256
C. Allison 1/26/76 9399256
D. Allison 1/26/75 9993356

2.____

3. Farrell 2/12/75 361251

A. Farell 2/21/75 361251
B. Farrell 2/12/75 361251
C. Farrell 2/21/75 361251
D. Farrell 2/12/75 361151

3.____

4. Guerrero 4/28/72 105689
    A. Guererro 4/28/72 105689
    B. Guerrero 4/28/72 105986
    C. Guerrero 4/28/72 105869
    D. Guerrero 4/28/72 105689

    4.____

5. McDonnell 6/05/73 478215
    A. McDonnell 6/15/73 478215
    B. McDonnell 6/05/73 478215
    C. McDonnell 6/05/73 472815
    D. MacDonell 6/05/73 478215

    5.____

6. Shepard 3/31/71 075421
    A. Sheperd 3/31/71 075421
    B. Shepard 3/13/71 075421
    C. Shepard 3/31/71 075421
    D. Shepard 3/13/71 075241

    6.____

7. Russell 4/01/69 031429
    A. Russell 4/01/69 031429
    B. Russell 4/10/69 034129
    C. Russell 4/10/69 031429
    D. Russell 4/01/69 034129

    7.____

8. Phillips 10/16/68 961042
    A. Philipps 10/16/68 961042
    B. Phillips 10/16/68 960142
    C. Phillips 10/16/68 961042
    D. Philipps 10/16/68 916042

    8.____

9. Campbell 11/21/72 624856
    A. Campbell 11/21/72 624856
    B. Campbell 11/21/72 624586
    C. Campbell 11/21/72 624686
    D. Campbel 11/21/72 624856

    9.____

10. Patterson 9/18/71 76199176
    A. Patterson 9/18/72 76191976
    B. Patterson 9/18/71 76199176
    C. Patterson 9/18/72 76199176
    D. Patterson 9/18/71 76919176

    10.____

Questions 11-15.

DIRECTIONS: Questions 11 through 15 consist of groups of numbers and letters which you are to compare. For each question, you are to choose the option (A, B, C, or D) in Column I which EXACTLY matches the group of numbers and letters given in Column I.

SAMPLE QUESTION

Column I
B92466

Column II
A. B92644
B. B94266
C. A92466
D. B92466

3 (#1)

The correct answer is D. Only Option D in Column II shows the group of numbers and letters EXACTLY as it appears in Column I. Now answer Questions 11 through 15 in the same manner.

	Column I		Column II	
11.	925AC5	A. 952CA5 B. 925AC5 C. 952AC5 D. 925CA6		11.____
12.	Y006925	A. Y060925 B. Y006295 C. Y006529 D. Y006925		12.____
13.	J236956	A. J236956 B. J326965 C. J239656 D. J932656		13.____
14.	AB6952	A. AB6952 B. AB9625 C. AB9652 D. AB6925		14.____
15.	X259361	A. X529361 B. X259631 C. X523961 D. X259361		15.____

Questions 16-25.

DIRECTIONS: Each of questions 16 through 25 consists of three lines of code letters and three lines of numbers. The numbers on each line should correspond with the code letters on the same line in accordance with the table below.

Code Letter	S	V	W	A	Q	M	X	E	G	K
Corresponding Number	0	1	2	3	4	5	5	7	8	9

On some of the lines, an error exists in the coding. Compare the letters and numbers in each question carefully. If you find an error or errors on:
    only one of the lines in the question, mark your answer A;
    any two lines in the question, mark your answer B;
    all three lines in the question, mark your answer C;
    none of the lines in the question, mark your answer D.

4 (#1)

SAMPLE QUESTION

    WQGKSXG   2489068
    XEKVQMA   6591453
    KMAESXV   9527061

In the above sample, the first line is correct since each code letter listed has the correct corresponding number. On the second line, an error exists because code letter E should have the number 7 instead of the number 5. On the third line, an error exists because the code letter A should have the number 3 instead of the number 2. Since there are errors in two of the three lines, the correct answer is B. Now answer Questions 16 through 25 in the same manner.

16. SWQEKGA   0247983   16._____
      KEAVSXM   9731065
      SSAXGKQ   0036894

17. QAMKMVS   4259510   17._____
      MGGEASX   5897306
      KSWMKWS   9125920

18. WKXQWVE   2964217   18._____
      QKXXQVA   4966413
      AWMXGVS   3253810

19. GMMKASE   8559307   19._____
      AWVSKSW   3210902
      QAVSVGK   4310189

20. XGKQSMK   6894049   20._____
      QSVKEAS   4019730
      GSMXKMV   8057951

21. AEKMWSG   3195208   21._____
      MKQSVQK   5940149
      XGQAEVW   6843712

22. XGMKAVS   6858310   22._____
      SKMAWEQ   0953174
      GVMEQSA   8167403

23. VQSKAVE   1489317   23._____
      WQGKAEM   2489375
      MEGKAWQ   5689324

24. XMQVSKG   6541098   24._____
      QMEKEWS   4579720
      KMEVGKG   9571983

25. GKVAMEW   88912572   25._____
    AXMVKAE   3651937
    KWAGMAV   9238531

Questions 26-35.

DIRECTIONS: Each of Questions 26 through 35 consists of a column of figures. For each question, add the column of figures and choose the correct answer from the four choices given.

26. 5,665.43   26._____
     2,356.69
     6,447.24
     7,239.65

   A. 20,698.01   B. 21,709.01
   C. 21,718.01   D. 22,609.01

27. 817,209.55   27._____
     264,354.29
      82,368.76
     849,964.89

   A. 1,893.977.49   B. 1,989,988.39
   C. 2,009,077.39   D. 2,013,897.49

28. 156,366.89   28._____
     249,973.23
     823,229.49
      56,869.45

   A. 1,286,439.06   B. 1,287,521.06
   C. 1,297,539.06   D. 1,296,421.06

29.   23,422.15   29._____
     149,696.24
     238,377.53
      86,289.79
     505,533.63

   A. 989,229.34   B. 999,879.34
   C. 1,003,330.34   D. 1,023,329.34

6 (#1)

30.   2,468,926.70
      656,842.28
        49,723.15
      832,369.59

    A. 3,218,062.72   B. 3,808,092.72
    C. 4,007,861.72   D. 4,818,192.72

30.____

31.   524,201.52
    7,775,678.51
    8,345,299.63
  40,628,898.08
  31,374,670.07

    A. 88,646,647.81   B. 88,646,747.91
    C. 88,648,647.91   D. 88,648,747.81

31.____

32.   6,824,829.40
     682,482.94
  5,542,015.27
     775,678.51
  7,732,507.25

    A. 21,557,513.37   B. 21,567,513.37
    C. 22,567,503.37   D. 22,567,513.37

32.____

33.   22,109,405.58
    6,097,093.43
    5,050,073.99
    8,118,050.05
    4,313,980.82

    A. 45,688,593.87   B. 45,688,603.87
    C. 45,689,593.87   D. 45,689,603.87

33.____

34.   79,324,114.19
    99,848,129.74
    43,331,653.31
    41,610,207.14

    A. 264,114,104.38   B. 264,114,114.38
    C. 265,114,114.38   D. 265,214,104.38

34.____

35. 33,729,653.94
      5,959,342.58
     26,052,715.47
      4,452,669.52
      7,079,953.59

   A. 76,374,334.10   B. 76,375,334.10
   C. 77,274,335.10   D. 77,275,335.10

Questions 36-40.

DIRECTIONS: Each of Questions 36 through 40 consists of a single number in Column I and four options in Column II. For each question, you are to choose the option (A, B, C, or D) in Column II which EXACTLY matches the number in Column I.

SAMPLE QUESTION

Column I   Column II
5965121   A. 5956121
                 B. 5965121
                 C. 5966121
                 D. 5965211

The correct answer is B. Only Option B shows the number EXACTLY as it appears in Column I. Now answer Questions 36 through 40 in the same manner.

	Column I	Column II
36.	9643242	A. 9643242 B. 9462342 C. 9642442 D. 9463242
37.	3572477	A. 3752477 B. 3725477 C. 3572477 D. 3574277
38.	5276101	A. 5267101 B. 5726011 C. 5271601 D. 5276101
39.	4469329	A. 4496329 B. 4469329 C. 4496239 D. 4469239

40. 2326308   A. 2236308   40.____
                    B. 2233608
                    C. 2326308
                    D. 2323608
                    _____

KEY (CORRECT ANSWERS)

1.	D	11.	B	21.	A	31.	D
2.	A	12.	D	22.	C	32.	A
3.	B	13.	A	23.	B	33.	B
4.	D	14.	A	24.	D	34.	A
5.	B	15.	D	25.	A	35.	C
6.	C	16.	D	26.	B	36.	A
7.	A	17.	C	27.	D	37.	C
8.	C	18.	A	28.	A	38.	D
9.	A	19.	D	29.	C	39.	B
10.	B	20.	B	30.	C	40.	C

TEST 2

DIRECTIONS: Each question or incomplete statement is followed by several suggested answers or completions. Select the one that BEST answers the question or completes the statement. *PRINT THE LETTER OF THE CORRECT ANSWER IN THE SPACE AT THE RIGHT.*

Questions 1-5.

DIRECTIONS: Each of Questions 1 through 5 consists of a name and a dollar amount. In each question, the name and dollar amount in Column II should be an EXACT copy of the name and dollar amount in Column I. If there is:
  a mistake only in the name, mark your answer A;
  a mistake only in the dollar amount, mark your answer B;
  a mistake in both the name and the dollar amount, mark your answer C;
  no mistake in either the name or the dollar amount, mark your answer D.

SAMPLE QUESTION

Column I	Column II
George Peterson	George Petersson
$125.50	$125.50

Compare the name and dollar amount in Column II with the name and dollar amount in Column I. The name *Petersson* in Column II is spelled *Peterson* in Column I. The amount is the same in both columns. Since there is a mistake only in the name, the answer to the sample question is A. Now answer Questions 1 through 5 in the same manner.

	Column I	Column II	
1.	Susanne Shultz $3440	Susanne Schultz $3440	1.____
2.	Anibal P. Contrucci $2121.61	Anibel P. Contrucci $2112.61	2.____
3.	Eugenio Mendoza $12.45	Eugenio Mendozza $12.45	3.____
4.	Maurice Gluckstadt $4297	Maurice Gluckstadt $4297	4.____
5.	John Pampellonne $4656.94	John Pammpellonne $4566.94	5.____

125

Questions 6-11.

DIRECTIONS: Each of Questions 6 through 11 consist of a set of names and addresses, which you are to compare. In each question, the name and addresses in Column II should be an EXACT copy of the name and address in Column I. If there is:
- a mistake only in the name, mark your answer A;
- a mistake only in the address, mark your answer B;
- a mistake in both the name and address, mark your answer C;
- no mistake in either the name or address, mark your answer D.

SAMPLE QUESTION

Column I	Column II
Michael Filbert	Michael Filbert
456 Reade Street	645 Reade Street
New York, N.Y. 10013	New York, N.Y. 10013

Since there is a mistake only in the address (the street number should be 456 instead of 645), the answer to the sample question is B. Now answer Questions 6 through 11 in the same manner.

	Column I	Column II	
6.	Hilda Goettelmann 55 Lenox Rd. Brooklyn, N.Y. 11226	Hilda Goetteleman 55 Lenox Ave. Brooklyn, N.Y. 11226	6.____
7.	Arthur Sherman 2522 Batchelder St. Brooklyn, N.Y. 11235	Arthur Sharman 2522 Batcheder St. Brooklyn, N.Y. 11253	7.____
8.	Ralph Barnett 300 West 28 Street New York, New York 10001	Ralph Barnett 300 West 28 Street New York, New York 10001	8.____
9.	George Goodwin 135 Palmer Avenue Staten Island, New York 10302	George Godwin 135 Palmer Avenue Staten Island, New York 10302	9.____
10.	Alonso Ramirez 232 West 79 Street New York, N.Y. 10024	Alonso Ramirez 223 West 79 Street New York, N.Y. 10024	10.____
11.	Cynthia Graham 149-34 83 Street Howard Beach, N.Y. 11414	Cynthia Graham 149-35 83 Street Howard Beach, N.Y. 11414	11.____

Questions 12-20.

DIRECTIONS: Questions 12 through 20 are problems in subtraction. For each question do the subtraction and select your answer from the four choices given.

12. 232,921.85
    -179,587.68

    A. 52,433.17   B. 52,434.17
    C. 53,334.17   D. 53,343,17

    12.____

13. 5,531,876.29
    -3,897,158.36

    A. 1,634,717.93   B. 1,644,718.93
    C. 1,734,717.93   D. 1,7234,718.93

    13.____

14. 1,482,658.22
    -937,925.76

    A. 544,633.46   B. 544,732.46
    C. 545,632.46   D. 545,732.46

    14.____

15. 937,828.17
    -259,673.88

    A. 678,154.29   B. 679,154.29
    C. 688,155.39   D. 699,155.39

    15.____

16. 760,412.38
    -263,465.95

    A. 496,046.43   B. 496,946.43
    C. 496,956.43   D. 497,046.43

    16.____

17. 3,203,902.26
    -2,933,087.96

    A. 260,814.30   B. 269,824.30
    C. 270,814.30   D. 270,824.30

    17.____

18. 1,023,468.71
    -934,678.88

    A. 88,780.83   B. 88,789.83
    C. 88,880.83   D. 88,889.83

    18.____

4 (#2)

19. 831,549.47
    -772,814.78

    A. 58,734.69
    C. 59,735.69
    B. 58,834.69
    D. 59,834.69

    19._____

20. 6,306,181.74
    -3,617,376.99

    A. 2,687,904.99
    C. 2,689,804.99
    B. 2,688,904.99
    D. 2,799,905.99

    20._____

Questions 21-30.

DIRECTIONS: Each of Questions 21 through 30 consists of three lines of code letters and three lines of numbers. The numbers on each line should correspond with the code letters on the same line in accordance with the table below.

Code Letter	J	U	B	T	Y	D	K	R	L	P
Corresponding Number	0	1	2	3	4	5	5	7	8	9

On some of the lines, an error exists in the coding. Compare the letters and numbers in each question carefully. If you find an error or errors on:
only *one* of the lines in the question, mark your answer A;
any *two* lines in the question, mark your answer B;
all *three* lines in the question, mark your answer C;
none of the lines in the question, mark your answer D.

SAMPLE QUESTION

BJRPYUR   2079417
DTBPYKJ   5328460
YKLDBLT   4685283

In the above sample, the first line is correct since each code letter listed has the correct corresponding number. On the second line, an error exists because code letter P should have the number 9 instead of the number 8. The third line is correct since each code letter listed has the correct corresponding number. Since there is an error in *one* of the three lines, the correct answer is A. Now answer Questions 21 through 30 in the same manner.

21. BYPDTJL   2495308
    PLRDTJU   9815301
    DTJRYLK   5207486

    21._____

22. RPBYRJK   7934706
    PKTYLBU   9624821
    KDLPJYR   6489047

    22._____

5 (#2)

23.	TPYBUJR	3942107	23.____
	BYRKPTU	2476931	
	DUKPYDL	5169458	
24.	KBYDLPL	6345898	24.____
	BLRKBRU	2876261	
	JTULDYB	0318542	
25.	LDPYDKR	8594567	25.____
	BDKDRJL	2565708	
	BDRPLUJ	2679810	
26.	PLRLBPU	9858291	26.____
	LPYKRDJ	88936750	
	TDKPDTR	3569527	
27.	RKURPBY	7617924	27.____
	RYUKPTJ	7426930	
	RTKPTJD	7369305	
28.	DYKPBJT	5469203	28.____
	KLPJBTL	6890238	
	TKPLBJP	3698209	
29.	BTPRJYL	2397148	29.____
	LDKUTYR	8561347	
	YDBLRPJ	4528190	
30.	ULPBKYT	1892643	30.____
	KPDTRBJ	6953720	
	YLKJPTB	4860932	

KEY (CORRECT ANSWERS)

1.	A	11.	D	21.	B
2.	C	12.	C	22.	C
3.	A	13.	A	23.	D
4.	D	14.	B	24.	B
5.	C	15.	A	25.	A
6.	C	16.	B	26.	C
7.	C	17.	C	27.	A
8.	D	18.	B	28.	D
9.	A	19.	A	29.	B
10.	B	20.	B	30.	D

BASIC FUNDAMENTALS OF FILING SCIENCE

TABLE OF CONTENTS

	Page
I. COMMENTARY	1
II. BASICS OF FILING	1
1. Types of Files	1
a. Shannon File	1
b. Spindle File	1
c. Box File	1
d. Flat File	1
e. Bellows File	1
f. Vertical File	1
g. Clip File	1
h. Visible File	2
i. Rotary File	2
2. Aids in Filing	2
3. Variations of Filing Systems	2
4. Centralized Filing	2
5. Methods of Filing	3
a. Alphabetic Filing	3
b. Subject Filing	3
c. Geographical Filing	3
d. Chronological Filing	3
e. Numerical Filing	3
6. Indexing	3
7. Alphabetizing	4
III. RULES FOR INDEXING AND ALPHABETIZING	4
IV. OFFICIAL EXAMINATION DIRECTIONS AND RULES	8
1. Official Directions	8
2. Official Rules For Alphabetical Filing	9
a. Names of Individuals	9
b. Names of Business Organizations	9
3. Sample Question	9

BASIC FUNDAMENTALS OF FILING SCIENCE

I. COMMENTARY

Filing is the systematic arrangement and storage of papers, cards, forms, catalogues, etc. so that they may be found easily and quickly. The importance of an efficient filing system cannot be emphasized too strongly. The filed materials form records which may be needed quickly to settle questions that may cause embarrassing situations if such evidence is not available. In addition to keeping papers in order so that they are readily available, the filing system must also be designed to keep papers in good condition. A filing system must be planned so that papers may be filed easily, withdrawn easily, and as quickly returned to their proper place. The cost of a filing system is also an important factor

The need for a filing system arose when the businessman began to carry on negotiations on a large scale. He could no longer be intimate with the details of his business. What was needed in the early era was a spindle or pigeon-hole desk. Filing in pigeon-hole desks is now almost completely extinct. It was an unsatisfactory practice since pigeon holes were not labeled, and the desk was an untidy mess.

II. BASIS OF FILING

The science of filing is an exact one and entails a thorough understanding of basic facts, materials, and methods. An overview of this important information now follows.

1. Types of Files

    a. Shannon File: This consists of a board, at one end of which are fastened two arches which may be opened laterally.

    b. Spindle File: This consists of a metal or wood base to which is attached a long, pointed spike. Papers are pushed down on the spike as received. This file is useful for temporary retention of papers.

    c. Box File: This is a heavy cardboard or metal box, opening from the side like a book.

    d. Flat File: This consists of a series of shallow drawers or trays, arranged like drawers in a cabinet.

    e. Bellows File: This is a heavy cardboard container with alphabetized or compartment sections, the ends of which are enclosed in such a manner that they resemble an accordion.

    f. Vertical File: This consists of one or more drawers in which the papers are stood on edge, usually in folders, and are indexed by guides. A series of two or more drawers in one unit is the usual file cabinet.

    g. Clip File: This file has a large clip attached to a board and is very similar to the Shannon File.

h. Visible File: Cards are filed flat in an overlapping arrangement which leaves a part of each card visible at all times.

i. Rotary File: The rotary file has a number of visible card files attached to a post around which they can be revolved. The wheel file has visible cards which rotate around a horizontal axis.

j. Tickler File: This consists of cards or folders marked with the days of the month, in which materials are filed and turned up on the appropriate day of the month.

2. Aids in Filing

   a. Guides: Guides are heavy cardboard, pasteboard, or Bristol-board sheets the same size as folders. At the top is a tab on which is marked or printed the distinguishing letter, words, or numbers indicating the material filed in a section of the drawer.

   b. Sorting Trays: Sorting trays are equipped with alphabetical guides to facilitate the sorting of papers preparatory to placing them in a file.

   c. Coding: Once the classification or indexing caption has been determined, it must be indicated on the letter for filing purposes.

   d. Cross-Reference: Some letters or papers might easily be called for under two or more captions. For this purpose, a cross-reference card or sheet is placed in the folder or in the index.

3. Variations of Filing Systems

   a. Variadex Alphabetic Index: Provides for more effective expansion of the alphabetic system.

   b. Triple-Check Numeric Filing: Entails a multiple cross-reference, as the name implies.

   c. Variadex Filing: Makes use of color as an aid in filing.

   d. Dewey Decimal System: The system is a numeric one used in libraries or for filing library materials in an office. This special type of filing system is used where material is grouped in finely divided categories, such as in libraries. With this method, all material to be filed is divided into ten major groups, from 000 to 900, and then subdivided into tens, units, and decimals.

4. Centralized Filing

Centralized filing means keeping the files in one specific or central location. Decentralized filing means putting away papers in files of individual departments. The first step in the organization of a central filing department is to make a careful canvass of all desks in the offices. In this manner we can determine just what material needs to be filed, and what information each desk occupant requires from the central file. Only papers which may be used at some time by persons in the various offices should be placed in the central file. A paper that is to be used at some time by persons in the various offices should be placed in the central file. A paper that is to be used by one department only should never be filed in the central file.

5. Methods of Filing

   While there are various methods used for filing, actually there are only five basic systems: alphabetical, subject, numerical, geographic, and chronological. All other systems are derived from one of these or from a combination of two or more of them. Since the purpose of a filing system is to store business records systemically so that any particular record can be found almost instantly when required, filing requires, in addition to the proper kinds of equipment and supplies, an effective method of indexing.
   There are five basic systems of filing:

   a. Alphabetic Filing: Most filing is alphabetical. Other methods, as described below, require extensive alphabetization. In alphabetical filing, lettered dividers or guides are arranged in alphabetic sequence. Material to be filed is placed behind the proper guide. All materials under each letter are also arranged alphabetically. Folders are used unless the file is a card index.

   b. Subject Filing: This method is used when a single, complete file on a certain subject is desired. A subject file is often maintained to assemble all correspondence on a certain subject. Such files are valuable in connection with insurance claims, contract negotiations, personnel, and other investigations, special programs, and similar subjects.

   c. Geographical File: Materials are filed according to location: states, cities, counties, or other subdivisions. Statistics and tax information are often filed in this manner.

   d. Chronological File: Records are filed according to date. This method is used especially in "tickler" files that have guides numbered 1 to 31 for each day of the month. Each number indicates the day of the month when the filed item requires attention.

   e. Numerical File: This method requires an alphabetic card index giving name and number. The card index is used to locate records numbered consecutively in the files according to date received or sequence in which issued, such as licenses, permits, etc.

6. Indexing

   Determining the name or title under which an item is to be filed is known as indexing. For example, how would a letter from Robert E. Smith be filed? The name would be rearranged Smith, Robert E., so that the letter would be filed under the last name.

7. Alphabetizing

The arranging of names for filing is known as alphabetizing. For example, suppose you have four letters indexed under the names Johnson, Becker, Roe, and Stern. How should these letters be arranged in the files so that they may be found easily? You would arrange the four names alphabetically, thus Becker, Johnson, Roe, and Stern.

III. RULES FOR INDEXING AND ALPHABETIZING

1. The names of persons are to be transposed. Write the surname first, then the given name, and, finally, the middle name or initial. Then arrange the various names according to the alphabetic order of letters throughout the entire name. If there is a title, consider that after the middle name or initial.

NAMES	INDEXED AS
Arthur L. Bright	Bright, Arthur L.
Arthur S. Bright	Bright, Arthur S.
P.E. Cole	Cole, P.E.
Dr. John C. Fox	Fox, John C. (Dr.)

2. If a surname includes the same letters of another surname, with one or more additional letters added to the end, the shorter surname is placed first regardless of the given name or the initial of the given name.

NAMES	INDEXED AS
Robert E. Brown	Brown, Robert E.
Gerald A. Browne	Browne, Gerald A.
William O. Brownell	Brownell, William O.

3. Firm names are alphabetized under the surnames. Words like the, an, a, of, and for, are not considered.

NAMES	INDEXED AS
Bank of America	Bank of America
Bank Discount Dept.	Bank Discount Dept.
The Cranford Press	Cranford Press, The
Nelson Dwyer & Co.	Dwyer, Nelson, & Co.
Sears, Roebuck & Co.	Sears Roebuck & Co.
Montgomery Ward & Co.	Ward, Montgomery, & Co.

4. The order of filing is determined first of all by the first letter of the names to be filed. If the first letters are the same, the order is determined by the second letters, and so on. In the following pairs of names, the order is determined by the letters underlined:

   A__u__sten   Ha__y__es   Han__s__on   Har__v__ey   Heat__h__   Gree__n__   Schw__a__rtz
   B__a__ker   He__a__th   Har__p__er   Har__w__ood   Hea__t__on   Greene   Schwar__z__

5. When surnames are alike, those with initials only precede those with given names, unless the first initial comes alphabetically after the first letter of the name.

   Gleason, S.   *but*, Abbott, Mary
   Gleason, S.W.   Abbott, W.B.
   Gleason, Sidney

6. Hyphenated names are treated as if spelled without the hyphen.
   - Lloyd, Paul N.
   - Lloyd-Jones, James
   - Lloyd, Robert
   - Lloyd-Thomas, A.S.

7. Company names composed of single letters which are not used as abbreviations precede the other names beginning with the same letter.
   - B & S Garage
   - B X Cable Co.
   - Babbitt, R.N.
   - E Z Duplicator Co.
   - Eagle Typewriter Co.
   - Edison Company

8. The ampersand (&) and the apostrophe (') in firm names are disregarded in alphabetizing.
   - Nelson & Niller
   - Nelson, Walter J.
   - Nelson's Bakery
   - M & C Amusement Corp.
   - M C Art Assn.

9. Names beginning with Mac, Mc, or M' are usually placed in regular order as spelled. Some filing systems file separately names beginning with Mc.
   - MacDonald, R.J.
   - MacDonald, S.B.
   - Mace, Wm.
   - Mazza, Anthony
   - McAdam, Wm.
   - McAndrews, Jerry

10. Names beginning with St. are listed as if the name Saint were spelled in full. Numbered street names and all abbreviated names are treated as if spelled out in full.
    - Saginaw
    - St. Louis
    - St. Peter's Rectory
    - Sandford
    - Smith, Wm.
    - Smith, Willis
    - Fifth Avenue Hotel
    - 42nd Street Dress Shop
    - Hart, Chas.
    - Hart, Charlotte
    - Hart, Jas.
    - Hart, Janice
    - Hart Mfg. Co.
    - Hart, Martin
    - Hart, Thos.
    - Hart, Thomas A.
    - Hart, Thos. R.

11. Federal, state, or city departments of government should be placed alphabetically under the governmental branch controlling them.
    - Illinois, State of – Departments and Commissions
      - Banking Dept.
      - Employment Bureau
    - United States Government Departments
      - Commerce
      - Defense
      - State
      - Treasury

12. Alphabetic Order: Each word in a name is an indexing unit. Arrange the names in alphabetic order by comparing similar units in each name. Consider the second units only when the first units are identical. Consider the third units only when both the first and second units are identical.

13. Single Surnames or Initials: A surname, when used alone, precedes the same surname with a first name or initial. A surname with a first initial only precedes a surname with a complete first name. This rule is sometimes stated, "nothing comes before something."

14. Surname Prefixes: A surname prefix is not a separate indexing unit, but it is considered part of the surname. These prefixes include: d', D', Da, de, De, Del, Des, Di, Du, Fitz., La, Le, Mc, Mac, 'c, O', St., Van, Van der, Von, Von der, and others. The prefixes M', Mac, and Mc are indexed and filed exactly as they are spelled.

15. Names of Firms: Names of firms and institutions are indexed and filed exactly as they are written when they do not contain the complete name of an individual.

16. Names of Firms Containing Complete Individual Names: When the firm or institution name includes the complete name of an individual, the units are transposed for indexing in the same way as the name of an individual.

17. Article "The": When the article "the" occurs at the beginning of a name, it is placed at the end in parentheses but it is not moved. In both cases, it is not an indexing unit and is disregarded in filing.

18. Hyphenated Names: Hyphenated firm names are considered as separate indexing units. Hyphenated surnames of individuals are considered as one indexing unit; this applies also to hyphenated names of individuals whose complete names are part of a firm name.

19. Abbreviations: Abbreviations are considered as though the name were written in full; however, single letters other than abbreviations are considered as separate indexing units.

20. Conjunctions, Prepositions, and Firm Endings: Conjunctions and prepositions, such as and, for, in, of, are disregarded in indexing and filing but are not omitted or their order changed when writing names on cards and folders. Firm endings, such as Ltd., Inc., So., Son, Bros., Mfg., and Corp. , are treated as a unit in indexing and filing and are considered as though spelled in full, such as Brothers and Incorporated.

21. One of Two Words: Names that may be spelled either as one or two words are indexed and filed as one word.

22. Compound Geographic Names: Compound geographic names are considered as separate indexing and filing units, except when the first part of the name is not an English word, such as the Los in Los Angeles.

23. Titles or degrees of individuals, whether preceding or following the name, are not considered in indexing or filing. They are placed in parentheses after the given name or initial. Terms that designate seniority, such as Jr., Sr., 2d, are also placed in parentheses and are considered for indexing and filing only when the names to be indexed are otherwise identical.

Exception A: When the name of an individual consists of a title and one name only, such as Queen Elizabeth, it is not transposed and the title is considered for indexing and filing.
Exception B: When a title or foreign article is the initial word of a firm or association name, it is considered for indexing and filing.

24. Possessives: When a word ends in apostrophe s, the s is not considered in indexing and filing. However, when a word ends in s apostrophe, because the s is part of the original word, it is considered. This rule is sometimes stated, "Consider everything up to the apostrophe."

25. United States and Foreign Government Names: Names pertaining to the federal government are indexed and filed under United States Government and then subdivided by title of the department, bureau, division, commission, or board. Names pertaining to foreign governments are indexed and filed under names of countries and then subdivided by title of the department, bureau, division, commission, or board. Phrases, such as department of, bureau of, division of, commission of, board of, when used in titles of governmental bodies, are placed in parentheses after the word they modify, but are disregarded in indexing and filing. Such phrases, however, are considered in indexing and filing governmental names.

26. Other Political Subdivisions: Names pertaining to other political subdivisions, such as states, counties, cities, or towns, are indexed and filed under the name of the political subdivision and then subdivided by the title of the department, bureau, division, commission, or board.

27. When the same name appears with different addresses, the names are indexed as usual and arranged alphabetically according to city or town. The State is considered only when there is duplication of both individual or company name and city name. If the same name is located at different addresses within the same city, then the names are arranged alphabetically by streets. If the same name is located at more than one address on the same street then the names are arranged from the lower to the higher street number.

28. Numbers: Any number in a name is considered as though it were written in words, and it is indexed and filed as one unit.

29. Bank Names: Because the names of many banking institutions are alike in several respects, as First National Bank, Second National Bank, etc., banks are indexed and filed first by city location, then by bank name, with the state location written in parentheses and considered only if necessary.

30. Married Women: The legal name of a married woman is the one used for filing purposes. Legally, a man's surname is the only part of a man's name a woman assumes when she marries. Her legal name, therefore, could be either:
    a. Her own first and middle names together with her husband's surname, or
    b. Her own first name and maiden surname, together with her husband's surname.

Mrs. is placed in parentheses at the end of the name. Her husband's first and middle names are given in parentheses below her legal name.

31. An alphabetically arranged list of names illustrating many difficult points of alphabetizing follows:

COLUMN I	COLUMN II
Abbot, W.B.	54th St. Tailor Shop
Abbot, Alice	Forstall, W.J.
Allen Alexander B.	44th St. Garage
Allen, Alexander B., Inc.	M A Delivery Co.
Andersen, Hans	M & C Amusement Corp.
Andersen, Hans E.	M C Art Assn.
Andersen, Hans E., Jr.	MacAdam, Wm.
Anderson, Andrew Andrews,	Macaulay, James
George Brown Motor Co., Boston	MacAulay, Wilson
Brown Motor Co., Chicago	MacDonald, R.J.
Brown Motor Co., Philadelphia	Macdonald, S. B.
Brown Motor Co., San Francisco	Mace, Wm.
Dean, Anna	Mazza, Anthony
Dean, Anna F.	McAdam, Wm.
Dean, Anna Frances	McAndrews, Jerry
Dean & Co.	Meade & Clark Co.
Deane-Arnold Apartments	Meade, S.T.
Deane's Pharmacy	Meade, Soloman
Deans, Felix A.	Sackett Publishing Co.
Dean's Studio	Sacks, Robert
Deans, Wm.	St. Andrew Hotel
Deans & Williams	St. John, Homer W.
East Randolph	Saks, Isaac B.
East St. Louis	Stephens, Ira
Easton, Pa.	Stevens, Delevan
Eastport, Me.	Stevens, Delila

IV OFFICIAL EXAMINATION DIRECTIONS AND RULES

To preclude the possibility of conflicting or varying methods of filing, explicit directions and express rules are given to the candidate before he answers the filing questions on an examination.
The most recent official directions and rules for the filing questions are given immediately hereafter.

OFFICIAL DIRECTIONS

Each of questions...to...consists of four (five) names. For each question, select the one of the four(five) names that should be first (second)(third)(last) if the four (five(names were arranged in alphabetical order in accordance with the rules for alphabetical filing given below. Read these rules carefully. Then, for each question, indicate in the correspondingly numbered row on the answer sheet the letter preceding the name that should be first(second)(third)(last) in alphabetical order.

OFFICIAL RULES FOR ALPHABETICAL FILING

Names of Individuals

1. The names of individuals are filed in strict alphabetical order, first according to the last name, then according to first name or initial, and, finally, according to middle name or initial. For example: William Jones precedes George Kirk and Arthur S. Blake precedes Charles M. Blake.
2. When the last names are identical, the one with an initial instead of a first name precedes the one "with a first name beginning with the same initial." For example: J. Green precedes Joseph Green.
3. When identical last names also have identical first names, the one without a middle name or initial precedes the one with a middle name or initial. For example: Robert Jackson precedes both Robert C. Jackson and Robert Chester Jackson.
4. When last names are identical and the first names are also identical, the one with a middle initial precedes the one with a middle name beginning with the same initial. For example: Peter A. Brown precedes Peter Alvin Brown.
5. Prefixes such as De, El, La, and Van are considered parts of the names they precede. For example: Wilfred DeWald precedes Alexander Duval.
6. Last names beginning with "Mac" or "Mc" are filed as spelled.
7. Abbreviated names are treated as if they were spelled out. For example: Jos. is filed as Joseph and Robt. is filed as Robert.
8. Titles and designations such as Dr., Mrs., Prof. are disregarding in filing.

Names of Business Organizations

1. The names of business organizations are filed exactly as written, except that an organization bearing the name of an individual is filed alphabetically according to the name of the individual in accordance with the rules for filing names of individuals given above. For example: Thomas Allison Machine Company precedes Northern Baking Company.
2. When numerals occur in a name, they are treated as if they were spelled out. For example: 6 stands for six and 4th stands for fourth.
3. When the following words occur in names, they are disregarded: the, of

SAMPLE QUESTION

Choose the name that should be filed third.
A. Fred Town (2)   B. Jack Towne (3)   C. D. Town (1)   D. Jack Stone (4)
The numbers in parentheses indicate the proper alphabetical order in which these names should be filed. Since the name that should be filed third is Jack Towne, the answer is (B).

FILING

EXAMINATION SECTION
TEST 1

DIRECTIONS: Each question from 1 through 10 contains four names. For each question, choose the name that should be *FIRST* if the four names were arranged in alphabetical order in accordance with the Rules for Alphabetical Filing given before. Read these rules carefully. Then, for each question, print in the space at the right the letter before the name that should be *FIRST* in alphabetical order.

SAMPLE QUESTION
A. Jane Earl (2)
B. James A. Earle (4)
C. James Earl (1)
D. J. Earle (3)

The numbers in parentheses show the proper alphabetical order in which these names should be filed. Since the name that should be filed *FIRST* is James Earl, the answer to the sample question is C.

1. A. Majorca Leather Goods
    B. Robert Maiorca and Sons
    C. Maintenance Management Corp.
    D. Majestic Carpet Mills

2. A. Municipal Telephone Service
    B. Municipal Reference Library
    C. Municipal Credit Union
    D. Municipal Broadcasting System

3. A. Robert B. Pierce   B. R. Bruce Pierce
    C. Ronald Pierce   D. Robert Bruce Pierce

4. A. Four Seasons Sports Club
    B. 14 Street Shopping Center
    C. Forty Thieves Restaurant
    D. 42nd St. Theaters

5. A. Franco Franceschini   B. Amos Franchini
    C. Sandra Franceschia   D. Lilie Franchinesca

6. A. Chas. A. Levine   B. Kurt Levene
    C. Charles Levine   D. Kurt E. Levene

7. A. Prof. Geo. Kinkaid   B. Mr. Alan Kinkaid
    C. Dr. Albert A. Kinkade   D. Kincade Liquors Inc.

143

8. A. Department of Public Events   8.____
   B. Office of the Public Administrator
   C. Queensborough Public Library
   D. Department of Public Health

9. A. Martin Luther King, Jr. Towers   9.____
   B. Metro North Plaza
   C. Manhattanville Houses
   D. Marble Hill Houses

10. A. Dr. Arthur Davids   10.____
    B. The David Check Cashing Service
    C. A. C. Davidsen
    D. Milton Davidoff

KEY (CORRECT ANSWERS)

1. C
2. D
3. B
4. D
5. C

6. B
7. D
8. B
9. A
10. B

TEST 2

DIRECTIONS: Each of questions 1 to 10 consists of four names. For each question, select the one of the four names that should be *THIRD* if the four names were arranged in alphabetical order in accordance with the Rules of Alphabetical Filing given before. Read these rules carefully. Then, for each question, print in the space at the right the letter preceding the name that should be *THIRD* in alphabetical order.

SAMPLE QUESTION

    A. Fred Town (2)
    B. Jack Towne (3)
    C. D. Town (1)
    D. Jack S. Towne (4)

The numbers in parentheses indicate the proper alphabetical order in which these names should be filed. Since the name that should be filed *THIRD* is Jack Towne, the answer is B.

1.   A. Herbert Restman   B. H. Restman   1.____
    C. Harry Restmore   D. H. Restmore

2.   A. Martha Eastwood   B. Martha E. Eastwood   2.____
    C. Martha Edna Eastwood   D. M. Eastwood

3.   A. Timothy Macalan   B. Fred McAlden   3.____
    C. Thomas MacAllister   D. Mrs. Frank McAllen

4.   A. Elm Trading Co.   4.____
    B. El Dorado Trucking Corp.
    C. James Eldred Jewelry Store
    D. Eldridge Printing, Inc.

5.   A. Edward La Gabriel   B. Marie Doris Gabriel   5.____
    C. Marjorie N. Gabriel   D. Mrs. Marian Gabriel

6.   A. Peter La Vance   B. George Van Meer   6.____
    C. Wallace De Vance   D. Leonard Vance

7.   A. Fifth Avenue Book Shop   7.____
    B. Mr. Wm. A. Fifner
    C. 52nd Street Association
    D. Robert B. Fiffner

8.   A. Dr. Chas. D. Peterson   B. Miss Irene F. Petersen   8.____
    C. Lawrence E. Peterson   D. Prof. N. A. Petersen

9.   A. 71st Street Theater   B. The Seven Seas Corp.   9.____
    C. 7th Ave. Service Co.   D. Walter R. Sevan and Co.

10. A. Aerol Auto Body, Inc.
    B. AAB Automotive Service Corp.
    C. Acer Automotive
    D. Alerte Automotive Corp.

10.____

KEY (CORRECT ANSWERS)

1. D
2. B
3. B
4. D
5. C

6. D
7. A
8. A
9. C
10. A

TEST 3

DIRECTIONS: Same as for Test 2.

1. A. William Carver   B. Howard Cambell   1.____
   C. Arthur Chambers   D. Charles Banner

2. A. Paul Moore   B. William Moore   2.____
   C. Paul A. Moore   D. William Allen Moore

3. A. George Peters   B. Eric Petersen   3.____
   C. G. Peters   D. E. Petersen

4. A. Edward Hallam   B. Jos. Frank Hamilton   4.____
   C. Edward A. Hallam   D. Joseph F. Hamilton

5. A. Theodore Madison   B. Timothy McGill   5.____
   C. Thomas MacLane   D. Thomas A. Madison

6. A. William O'Hara   B. Arthur Gordon   6.____
   C. James DeGraff   D. Anne von Glatin

7. A. Charles Green   B. Chas. T. Greene   7.____
   C. Charles Thomas Greene   D. Wm. A. Greene

8. A. John Foss Insurance Co.   B. New World Stove Co.   8.____
   C. 14th Street Dress Shop   D. Arthur Stein Paper Co.

9. A. Gold Trucking Co.   B. B. 8th Ave. Garage   9.____
   C. The First National Bank   D. The Century Novelty Co.

10. A. F. L. Doskow   B. Natalie S. Doskow   10.____
    C. Samuel B. Doskow   D. Arthur G. Doskor

KEY (CORRECT ANSWERS)

1. A
2. B
3. D
4. D
5. D

6. A
7. C
8. B
9. C
10. B

TEST 4

DIRECTIONS: Each question from 1 through 10 consists of four names. For each question, choose the one of the four names that should be *LAST* if the four names were arranged in alphabetical order in accordance with the Rules for Alphabetical Filing given before. Read these rules carefully. Then, for each question, print in the space at the right the letter before the name that should be *LAST* in alphabetical order.

SAMPLE QUESTION

A. Jane Earl   (2)
B. James A. Earle (4)
C. James Earl   (1)
D. J. Earle   (3)

The numbers in parentheses show the proper alphabetical order in which these names should be filed. Since the name that should be filed *LAST* is James A. Earle, the answer to the sample question is B.

1. A. Corral, Dr. Robert   B. Carrale, Prof. Robert   1.___
    C. Corren, R.   D. Corret, Ron

2. A. Rivera, Ilena   B. Riviera, Ilene   2.___
    C. Rivere, I.   D. Riviera Ice-Cream Co.

3. A. VonHogel, George   B. Volper, Gary   3.___
    C. Vonner, G.   D. Van Pefel, Gregory

4. A. David Kallish Stationery Co.   4.___
    B. Emerson Microfilm Company
    C. David Kalder Industrial Engineers Associated
    D. 5th Avenue Office Furniture Co.

5. A. A. Bennet, C.   B. Benett, Chuck   5.___
    C. Bennet, Chas.   D. Bennett, Charles

6. A. The Board of Higher Education   6.___
    B. National Education Commission
    C. Eakin, Hugh
    D. Nathan, Ellen

7. A. McCloud, I.   B. MacGowen, Ian   7.___
    C. McGowen, Arthur   D. Macale, Sean

8. A. Devine, Sarah   B. Devine, S.   8.___
    C. Devine, Sara H.   D. Devin, Sarah

9. A. Milstein, Louis   B. Milrad, Abraham P.   9.___
    C. Milstein, Herman   D. Milstien, Harold G.

10. A. Herfield, Lester L.   B. Herbstman, Nathan   10.___
    C. Henricksen, Ole A.   D. Herfeld, Burton G.

KEY (CORRECT ANSWERS)

1. D
2. B
3. C
4. A
5. D

6. B
7. C
8. A
9. D
10. A

TEST 5

DIRECTIONS: Same as for Test 4.

1. A. Francis Lattimore B. H. Latham 1.____
   C. G. Lattimore D. Hugh Latham

2. A. Thomas B. Morgan B. B. Thomas Morgan 2.____
   C. T. Morgan D. Thomas Bertram Morgan

3. A. Lawrence A. Villon B. Chas. Valente 3.____
   C. Charles M. Valent D. Lawrence De Villon

4. A. Alfred Devance B. A. R. D'Amico 4.____
   C. Arnold De Vincent D. A. De Pino

5. A. Dr. Milton A. Bergmann B. Miss Evelyn M. Bergmenn 5.____
   C. Prof. E. N. Bergmenn D. Mrs. L. B. Bergmann

6. A. George MacDougald B. Thomas McHern 6.____
   C. William Macholt D. Frank McHenry

7. A. Third National Bank B. Robt. Tempkin Corp. 7.____
   C. 32nd Street Carpet Co. D. Wm. Templeton, Inc.

8. A. Mary Lobell Art Shop B. John La Marca, Inc 8.____
   C. Lawyers' Guild D. Frank Le Goff Studios

9. A. 9th Avenue Garage B. Jos. Nuren Food Co. 9.____
   C. The New Book Store D. Novelty Card Corp.

10. A. Murphy's Moving & Storage, Inc. 10.____
    B. Mid-Island Van Lines Corporation
    C. Mollone Bros. Moving & Storage, Inc.
    D. McShane Moving & Storage, Inc.

KEY (CORRECT ANSWERS)

1. C
2. D
3. A
4. C
5. B

6. B
7. C
8. A
9. B
10. A

TEST 6

DIRECTIONS: Each question contains four names numbered from 1 through 4 but not necessarily numbered in correct filing order. Answer each question by choosing the letter corresponding to the CORRECT filing order of the four names in accordance with the Rules for Alphabetic Filing given before. PRINT THE LETTER OF THE CORRECT ANSWER IN THE SPACE AT THE RIGHT.

SAMPLE QUESTION

1. Robert J. Smith
2. R. Jeffrey Smith
3. Dr. A. Smythe
4. Allen R. Smithers

A. 1, 2, 3, 4   B. 3, 1, 2, 4   C. 2, 1, 4, 3   D. 3, 2, 1, 4

Since the correct filing order, in accordance with the above rules, is 2, 1, 4, 3, the correct answer is C.

1. 1. J. Chester VanClief
   2. John C. VanClief
   3. J. VanCleve
   4. Mary L. Vance

   A. 4, 3, 1, 2   B. 4, 3, 2, 1   C. 3, 1, 2, 4   D. 3, 4, 1, 2

2. 1. Community Development Agency
   2. Department of Social Services
   3. Board of Estimate
   4. Bureau of Gas and Electricity

   A. 3, 4, 1, 2   B. 1, 2, 4, 3   C. 2, 1, 3, 4   D. 1, 3, 4, 2

3. 1. Dr. Chas. K. Dahlman
   2. F. & A. Delivery Service
   3. Department of Water Supply
   4. Demano Men's Custom Tailors

   A. 1, 2, 3, 4   B. 1, 4, 2, 3   C. 4, 1, 2, 3   D. 4, 1, 3, 2

4. 1. 48th Street Theater
   2. Fourteenth Street Day Care Center
   3. Professor A. Cartwright
   4. Albert F. McCarthy

   A. 4, 2, 1, 3   B. 4, 3, 1, 2   C. 3, 2, 1, 4   D. 3, 1, 2, 4

5. 1. Frances D'Arcy
   2. Mario L. DelAmato
   3. William H. Diamond
   4. Robert J. DuBarry

   A. 1, 2, 4, 3   B. 2, 1, 3, 4   C. 1, 2, 3, 4   D. 2, 1, 3, 4

6. 1. Evelyn H. D'Amelio
   2. Jane R. Bailey
   3. Robert Bailey
   4. Frank Baily

   A. 1, 2, 3, 4   B. 1, 3, 2, 4   C. 2, 3, 4, 1   D. 3, 2, 4, 1

7. 1. Department of Markets
   2. Bureau of Handicapped Children
   3. Housing Authority Administration Building
   4. Board of Pharmacy

2 (#6)

      A. 2,1,3,4   B. 1,2,4,3   C. 1,2,3,4   D. 3,2,1,4

8.   1. William A. Shea Stadium   8.____
     2. Rapid Speed Taxi Co.
     3. Harry Stampler's Rotisserie
     4. Wilhelm Albert Shea

      A. 2, 3, 4, 1   B. 4, 1, 3, 2   C. 2, 4, 1, 3   D. 3, 4, 1, 2

9.   1. Robert S. Aaron, M. D.   2. Mrs. Norma S. Aaron   9.____
     3. Irving I. Aronson   4. Darius P. Aanonsen

      A. 1, 2, 3, 4   B. 2, 4, 1, 3   C. 4, 2, 3, 1   D. 4, 2, 1, 3

10. 1. The Gamut   2. Gilliar Drug Co., Inc.   10.____
     3. Georgette Cosmetology   4. Great Nock Pharmacy

      A. 1, 3, 2, 4   B. 3, 1, 4, 2   C. 1, 2, 3, 4   D. 1, 3, 4, 2

KEY (CORRECT ANSWERS)

1. A
2. D
3. B
4. D
5. C

6. D
7. D
8. C
9. D
10. A

TEST 7

DIRECTIONS: Each question consists of four names grouped vertically under four different filing arrangements lettered A, B, C, and D. In each question only one of the four arrangements lists the names in the correct filing order according to the Rules for Alphabetical Filing given before. Read these rules carefully. Then, for each question, select the correct filing arrangement, lettered A, B, C, or D and print in the space at the right the letter of that correct filing arrangement.

SAMPLE QUESTION

Arrangement A
Arnold Robinson
Arthur Roberts
J. B. Robin
James Robin

Arrangement B
Arthur Roberts
J. B. Robin
James Robin
Arnold Robinson

Arrangement C
Arnold Robinson
Arthur Roberts
James Robin
J. B. Robin

Arrangement D
Arthur Roberts
James Robin
J. B. Robin
Arnold Robinson

Since, in this sample, ARRANGEMENT B is the only one in which the four names are correctly arranged alphabetically, the answer is B.

1. *Arrangement A*
   Alice Thompson
   Arnold G. Thomas
   B. Thomas
   Eugene Thompkins
   Arrangement C
   B. Thomas Arnold
   G. Thomas
   Eugene Thompkins
   Alice Thompson

   Arrangement B
   Eugene Thompkins
   Alice Thompson
   Arnold G. Thomas
   B. Thomas
   Arrangement D
   Arnold G. Thomas
   B. Thomas
   Eugene Thompkins
   Alice Thompson

   1.____

2. *Arrangement A*
   Albert Green
   A. B. Green
   Frank E. Green
   Wm. Greenfield
   Arrangement C
   Albert Green
   Wm. Greenfield
   A. B. Green
   Frank E. Green

   Arrangement B
   A. B. Green
   Albert Green
   Frank E. Green
   Wm. Greenfield
   Arrangement D
   A. B. Green
   Frank E. Green
   Albert Green
   Wm. Greenfield

   2.____

3. *Arrangement A*
   Steven M. Comte
   Robt. Count
   Robert B. Count
   Steven Le Comte
   Arrangement C
   Steven M. Comte
   Steven Le Comte
   Robt. Count
   Robert B. Count

   Arrangement B
   Steven Le Comte
   Steven M. Comte
   Robert B. Count
   Robt. Count
   Arrangement D
   Robt. Count
   Robert B. Count
   Steven Le Comte
   Steven M. Comte

   3.____

153

4. *Arrangement A*
   Prof. David Towner
   Miss Edna Tower
   Dr. Frank I. Tower
   Mrs. K. C. Towner
   Arrangement C
   Miss Edna Tower
   Dr. Frank I. Tower
   Prof. David Towner
   Mrs. K. C. Towner

   Arrangement B
   Dr. Frank I. Tower
   Miss Edna Tower
   Mrs. K. C. Towner
   Prof. David Towner
   Arrangement D
   Prof. David Towner
   Mrs. K. C. Towner
   Miss Edna Tower
   Dr. Frank I. Tower

4.____

5. *Arrangement A*
   The Jane Miller Shop
   Joseph Millard Corp.
   John Muller & Co.
   Jean Mullins, Inc.
   Arrangement C
   The Jane Miller Shop
   Jean Mullins, Inc.
   John Muller & Co.
   Joseph Millard Corp.

   Arrangement B
   Joseph Millard Corp.
   The Jane Miller Shop
   John Muller & Co.
   Jean Mullins, Inc.
   Arrangement D
   Joseph Millard Corp.
   John Muller & Co.
   Jean Mullins, Inc.
   The Jane Miller Shop

5.____

6. *Arrangement A*
   Anthony Delaney
   A. M. D'Elia
   A. De Landri
   Alfred De Monte
   Arrangement C
   A. De Landri
   A. M. D'Elia
   Alfred De Monte
   Anthony Delaney

   Arrangement B
   Anthony Delaney
   A. De Landri
   A. M. D'Elia
   Alfred De Monte
   Arrangement D
   A. De Landri
   Anthony Delaney
   A. M. D'Elia
   Alfred De Monte

6.____

7. *Arrangement A*
   D. McAllen
   Lewis McBride
   Doris MacAllister
   Lewis T. Mac Bride
   Arrangement C
   Doris MacAllister
   Lewis T. MacBride
   D. McAllen
   Lewis McBride

   Arrangement B
   D. McAllen
   Doris MacAllister
   Lewis McBride
   Lewis T. MacBride
   Arrangement D
   Doris MacAllister
   D. McAllen
   Lewis T. MacBride
   Lewis McBride

7.____

8. *Arrangement A*
    6th Ave. Swim Shop
    The Sky Ski School
    Sport Shoe Store
    23rd Street Salon
   Arrangement C
    6th Ave. Swim Shop
    Sport Shoe Store
    The Sky Ski School
    23rd Street Salon

   Arrangement B
    23rd Street Salon
    The Sky Ski School
    6th Ave. Swim Shop
    Sport Shoe Store
   Arrangement D
    The Sky Ski School
    6th Ave. Swim Shop
    Sport Shoe Store
    23rd Street Salon

   8.____

9. *Arrangement A*
    Charlotte Stair
    C. B. Stare
    Charles B. Stare
    Elaine La Stella
   Arrangement C
    Elaine La Stella
    Charlotte Stair
    C. B. Stare
    Charles B. Stare

   Arrangement B
    C. B. Stare
    Charles B. Stare
    Charlotte Stair
    Elaine La Stella
   Arrangement D
    Charles B. Stare
    C. B. Stare
    Charlotte Stair
    Elaine La Stella

   9.____

10. *Arrangement A*
    John O'Farrell Corp.
    Finest Glass Co.
    George Fraser Co.
    4th Guarantee Bank
   Arrangement C
    John O'Farrell Corp.
    Finest Glass Co.
    4th Guarantee Bank
    George Fraser Co.

   Arrangement B
    Finest Glass Co.
    4th Guarantee Bank
    George Fraser Co.
    John O'Farrell Corp.
   Arrangement D
    Finest Glass Co.
    George Fraser Co.
    John O'Farrell Corp.
    4th Guarantee Bank

   10.____

KEY (CORRECT ANSWERS)

1. D
2. B
3. A
4. C
5. B

6. D
7. C
8. A
9. C
10. B

TEST 8

DIRECTIONS: Same as for Test 7.

	Arrangement A	Arrangement B	Arrangement C	
1.	R. B. Stevens Chas. Stevenson Robert Stevens, Sr. Alfred T. Stevens	Alfred T. Stevens R. B. Stevens Robert Stevens, Sr. Chas. Stevenson	R. B. Stevens Robert Stevens, Sr. Alfred T. Stevens Chas. Stevenson	1.____
2.	Mr. A. T. Breen Dr. Otis C. Breen Amelia K. Brewington John Brewington	John Brewington Amelia K. Brewington Dr. Otis C. Breen Mr. A. T. Breen	Dr. Otis C. Breen Mr. A. T. Breen John Brewington Amelia K. Brewington	2.____
3.	J. Murphy J. J. Murphy John Murphy John J. Murphy	John Murphy John J. Murphy J. Murphy J. J. Murphy	J. Murphy John Murphy J. J. Murphy John J. Murphy	3.____
4.	Anthony DiBuono George Burns, Sr. Geo. T. Burns, Jr. Alan J. Byrnes	Geo. T. Burns, Jr. George Burns, Sr. Anthony DiBuono Alan J. Byrnes	George Burns, Sr. Geo. T. Burns, Jr. Alan J. Byrnes Anthony DiBuono	4.____
5.	James Macauley Frank A. McLowery Francis MacLaughry Bernard J. MacMahon	James Macauley Francis MacLoughry Bernard J. MacMahon Frank A. McLowery	Bernard J. MacMahon Francis MacLaughry Frank A. McLowery James Macauley	5.____
6.	A. J. DiBartolo, Sr. A. P. DiBartolo J. A. Bartolo Anthony J. Bartolo	J. A. Bartolo Anthony J. Bartolo A. P. DiBartolo A. J. DiBartolo, Sr.	Anthony J. Bartolo J. A. Bartolo A. J. DiBartolo, Sr. A. P. DiBartolo	6.____
7.	Edward Holmes Corp. Hillside Trust Corp. Standard Insurance Co. The Industrial Surety Co.	Edward Holmes Corp. Hillside Trust Corp. The Industrial Surety Co. Standard Insurance Co.	Hillside Trust Corp. Edward Holmes Corp. The Industrial Surety Co. Standard Insurance Co.	7.____
8.	Cooperative Credit Co. Chas. Cooke Chemical Corp. John Fuller Baking Co. 4th Avenue Express Co.	Chas. Cooke Chemical Corp. Cooperative Credit Co. 4th Avenue Express Co. John Fuller Baking Co.	4th Avenue Express Co. John Fuller Baking Co. Chas. Cooke Chemical Corp. Cooperative Credit Co.	8.____

2 (#8)

9.
   - Mr. R. McDaniels
   - Robert Darling, Jr.
   - F. L. Ramsey
   - Charles DeRhone

   - F. L. Ramsey
   - Mr. R. McDaniels
   - Charles DeRhone
   - Robert Darling, Jr.

   - Robert Darling, Jr. Charles DeRhone
   - Mr. R. McDaniels
   - F. L. Ramsey

   9.____

10.
    - New York Omnibus Corp.
    - New York Shipping Co.
    - Nova Scotia Canning Co.
    - John J. O'Brien Co.

    - John J. O'Brien Co.
    - New York Omnibus Corp.
    - New York Shipping Co.
    - Nova Scotia Caning Co.

    - Nova Scotia Canning Co.
    - John J. O'Brien Co.
    - New York Omnibus Corp.
    - New York Shipping Co.

    10.____

KEY (CORRECT ANSWERS)

1. B
2. A
3. A
4. C
5. B

6. C
7. C
8. B
9. C
10. A

TEST 9

DIRECTIONS: Each question consists of a group of names. Consider each group of names as a unit. Determine in what position the name printed in *ITALICS* would be if the names in the group were *CORRECTLY* arranged in alphabetical order. If the name in *ITALICS* should be first, print the letter A; if second, print the letter B; if third, print the letter C; if fourth, print the letter D; and if fifth, print the letter E. *PRINT THE LETTER OF THE CORRECT ANSWER IN THE SPACE AT THE RIGHT.*

SAMPLE QUESTION

J. W. Martin	2
James E. Martin	4
J. Martin	1
George Martins	5
James Martin	3

1. Albert Brown
   James Borenstein
   Frieda Albrecht
   Samuel Brown
   George Appelman

    1.____

2. James Ryan
   Francis Ryan
   Wm. Roanan
   Frances S. Ryan
   Francis P. Ryan

    2.____

3. Norman Fitzgibbons
   Charles F. Franklin
   Jas. Fitzgerald
   Andrew Fitzsimmons
   James P. Fitzgerald

    3.____

4. Hugh F. Martenson
   A. S. Martinson
   Albert Martinsen
   Albert S. Martinson
   M. Martanson

    4.____

5. Aaron M. Michelson
   Samuel Michels
   Arthur L. Michaelson, Sr.
   John Michell
   Daniel Michelsohn

    5.____

6. *Chas. R. Connolly* 6.____
   Frank Conlon
   Charles S. Connolly
   Abraham Cohen
   Chas. Conolly

7. James McCormack 7.____
   Ruth MacNamara
   Kathryn McGillicuddy
   Frances Mason
   Arthur MacAdams

8. Dr. Francis Karell 8.____
   John Joseph Karelsen, Jr. John J. Karelsen, Sr.
   Mrs. Jeanette Kelly
   Estelle Karel

9. *The 5th Ave. Bus Co.* 9.____
   The Baltimore and Ohio Railroad
   3rd Ave. Elevated Co.
   Pennsylvania Railroad
   The 4th Ave. Trolley Line

10. Murray B. Cunitz 10.____
    Cunningham Duct Cleaning Corp.
    James A. Cunninghame
    Jason M. Cuomor
    Talmadge L. Cummings

KEY (CORRECT ANSWERS)

1. E
2. D
3. A
4. E
5. D

6. C
7. C
8. D
9. B
10. C

TEST 10

DIRECTIONS: A supervisor who is responsible for the proper maintenance and operation of the filing system in an office of a depart-ment should be able to instruct and guide his subordinates in the correct filing of office records. The following ques-tions, 1 through 10, are designed to determine whether you can interpret and follow a prescribed filing procedure. These questions should be answered SOLELY on the basis of the fil-ing instructions which follow.

FILING INSTRUCTIONS FOR PERSONNEL DIVISION
DEPARTMENT X

The filing system of this division consists of three separate files, namely: (1) Employee File, (2) Subject File, (3) Correspondence File.

Employee File

This file contains a folder for each person currently employed in the department. Each report, memorandum, and letter which has been received from an official or employee of the department and which pertions to one employee only should be placed in the Employee File folder of the employee with whom the communication is concerned. (Note: This filing proce-dure also applies to a communication from a staff member who writes on a matter which con-cerns himself only.)

Subject File

Reports and memoranda originating in the department and dealing with personnel mat-ters affecting the entire staff or certain categories or groups of employees should be placed in the Subject File under the appropriate subject headings. The materials in this file are subdi-vided under the following five subject headings:

(1) Classification -- includes material on job analysis, change of title, reclassifica-tion of positions, etc.

(2) Employment -- includes material on appointment, promotion, re-instatement, and transfer.

(3) Health and Safety -- includes material dealing chiefly with the health and safety of employees.

(4) Staff Regulations -- includes material pertaining to rules and regulations gov-erning such working conditions as hours of work, lateness, vacation, leave of absence, etc.

(5) Training -- includes all material relating to employee training.

Correspondence File

All correspondence received from outside agencies, both public and private, and from persons outside the department, should be placed in the Correspondence File and cross ref-erenced as follows:

(1) When letters from outside agencies or persons relate to one or more employees currently employed in the department, a cross reference sheet should be placed in the Employee File folder of each employee mentioned.

(2) When letters from outside agencies or persons do not mention a specific employee or specific employees of the department, a cross reference sheet should be placed in the Subject File under the appropriate subject heading.

Questions 1-10 describe communications which have been received and acted upon by the Personnel Division of Department X, and which must be filed in accordance with the Filing Instructions for the Personnel Division.

The following filing operations may be performed in accordance with the above filing instructions:

- (A) Place in Employee File
- (B) Place in Subject File under Classification
- (C) Place in Subject File tinder Employment
- (D) Place in Subject File under Health and Safety
- (E) Place in Subject File under Staff Regulations
- (F) Place in Subject File under Training
- (G) Place in Correspondence File and cross reference in Employee File
- (H) Place in Correspondence File and cross reference in Subject File under Classification
- (I) Place in Correspondence File and cross reference in Subject File under Employment
- (J) Place in Correspondence File and cross reference in Subject File under Health and Safety
- (K) Place in Correspondence File and cross reference in Subject File under Staff Regulations
- (L) Place in Correspondence File and cross reference in Subject File under Training

DIRECTIONS: Examine each of questions 1 through 10 carefully. Then, in the space at the right, *print* the capital letter preceding the one of the filing operations listed above which MOST accurately carries out the Filing Instructions for the Personnel Division.

SAMPLE: A Clerk, Grade 2, in the department has sent in a memorandum requesting information regarding the amount of vacation due him.
The CORRECT answer is A.

1. Mr. Clark, a Clerk, Grade 5, has submitted an intradepartmental memorandum that the titles of all Clerks, Grade 5, in the department be changed to Administrative Assistant. 1.____

2. The secretary to the department has issued a staff order revising the schedule of Saturday work from a one-in-two to a one-in-four schedule. 2.____

3. The personnel officer of another agency has requested the printed transcripts of an in-service course recently conducted by the department. 3.____

4. Mary Smith, a secretary to one of the division chiefs, has sent in a request for a maternity leave of absence to begin on April 1 of this year and to terminate on March 31 of next year. 4.____

5. A letter has been received from a civic organization stating that they would like to know how many employees were promoted in the department during the last fiscal year. 5.____

6. The attorney for a municipal employees' organization has requested permission to represent Mr. James Roe, a departmental employee who is being brought up on charges of violating departmental regulations. 6.____

7. A letter has been received from Mr. Wright, a salesman for a paper company, who complains that Miss Jones, an information clerk in the department, has been rude and impertinent and has refused to give him information which should be available to the public. 7.____

8. Helen Brown, a graduate of Commercial High School, has sent a letter inquiring about an appointment as a provisional typist. 8.____

9. The National Office Managers' Society has sent a request to the department for information on its policies on tardiness and absenteeism. 9.____

10. A memorandum has been received from a division chief who states that employees in his unit have complained that their rest room is in a very unsanitary condition. 10.____

KEY (CORRECT ANSWERS)

1. B
2. E
3. L
4. A
5. I

6. G
7. G
8. I
9. K
10. D

NAME AND NUMBER COMPARISONS

COMMENTARY

This test seeks to measure your ability and disposition to do a job carefully and accurately, your attention to exactness and preciseness of detail, your alertness and versatility in discerning similarities and differences between things, and your power in systematically handling written language symbols.

It is actually a test of your ability to do academic and/or clerical work, using the basic elements of verbal (qualitative) and mathematical (quantitative) learning—words and numbers.

EXAMINATION SECTION

TEST 1

DIRECTIONS: In each line across the page there are three names or numbers that are much alike. Compare the three names or numbers and decide which ones are exactly alike. *PRINT IN THE SPACE AT THE RIGHT THE LETTER:*
  A. if all THREE names or numbers are exactly alike
  B. if only the FIRST and SECOND names or numbers are ALIKE
  C. if only the FIRST and THIRD names or numbers are alike
  D. if only the SECOND or THIRD names or numbers are alike
  E. if ALL THREE names or numbers are DIFFERENT

1.	Davis Hazen	David Hozen	David Hazen	1.____
2.	Lois Appel	Lois Appel	Lois Apfel	2.____
3.	June Allan	Jane Allan	Jane Allan	3.____
4.	10235	10235	10235	4.____
5.	32614	32164	32614	5.____

TEST 2

1.	2395890	2395890	2395890	1.____
2.	1926341	1926347	1926314	2.____
3.	E. Owens McVey	E. Owen McVey	E. Owen McVay	3.____
4.	Emily Neal Rouse	Emily Neal Rowse	Emily Neal Rowse	4.____
5.	H. Merritt Audubon	H. Merriott Audubon	H. Merritt Audubon	5.____

TEST 3

1.	6219354	6219354	6219354	1.____
2.	231793	2312793	2312793	2.____
3.	1065407	1065407	1065047	3.____
4.	Francis Ransdell	Frances Ramsdell	Francis Ramsdell	4.____
5.	Cornelius Detwiler	Cornelius Detwiler	Cornelius Detwiler	5.____

TEST 4

1.	6452054	6452564	6542054	1.____
2.	8501268	8501268	8501286	2.____
3.	Ella Burk Newham	Ella Burk Newnham	Elena Burk Newnham	3.____
4.	Jno. K. Ravencroft	Jno. H. Ravencroft	Jno. H. Ravencoft	4.____
5.	Martin Wills Pullen	Martin Wills Pulen	Martin Wills Pullen	5.____

TEST 5

1.	3457988	3457986	3457986	1.____
2.	4695682	4695862	4695682	2.____
3.	Stricklund Kaneydy	Sticklund Kanedy	Stricklund Kanedy	3.____
4.	Joy Harlor Witner	Joy Harloe Witner	Joy Harloe Witner	4.____
5.	R.M.O. Uberroth	R.M.O. Uberroth	R.N.O. Uberroth	5.____

3

TEST 6

1.	1592514	1592574	1592574	1.____
2.	2010202	2010202	2010220	2.____
3.	6177396	6177936	6177396	3.____
4.	Drusilla S. Ridgeley	Drusilla S. Ridgeley	Drusilla S. Ridgeley	4.____
5.	Andrei I. Tooumantzev	Andrei I. Tourmantzev	Andrei I. Toumantzov	5.____

TEST 7

1.	5261383	5261383	5261338	1.____
2.	8125690	8126690	8125609	2.____
3.	W.E. Johnston	W.E. Johnson	W.E. Johnson	3.____
4.	Vergil L. Muller	Vergil L. Muller	Vergil L. Muller	4.____
5.	Atherton R. Warde	Asheton R. Warde	Atherton P. Warde	5.____

TEST 8

1.	013469.5	023469.5	02346.95	1.____
2.	33376	333766	333766	2.____
3.	Ling-Temco-Vought	Ling-Tenco-Vought	Ling-Temco Vought	3.____
4.	Lorilard Corp.	Lorillard Corp.	Lorrilard Corp.	4.____
5.	American Agronomics Corporation	American Agronomics Corporation	American Agronomic Corporation	5.____

4

TEST 9

1.	436592864	436592864	436592864	1.____
2.	197765123	197755123	197755123	2.____
3.	Dewaay Cortvriendt International S.A.	Deway Cortvriendt International S.A.	Deway Corturiendt International S.A.	3.____
4.	Crédit Lyonnais	Crèdit Lyonnais	Crèdit Lyonais	4.____
5.	Algemene Bank Nederland N.V.	Algamene Bank Nederland N.V.	Algemene Bank Naderland N.V.	5.____

TEST 10

1.	00032572	0.0032572	00032522	1.____
2.	399745	399745	398745	2.____
3.	Banca Privata Finanziaria S.p.A.	Banca Privata Finanzaria S.P.A.	Banca Privata Finanziaria S.P.A.	3.____
4.	Eastman Dillon, Union Securities & Co.	Eastman Dillon, Union Securities Co.	Eastman Dillon, Union Securities & Co.	4.____
5.	Arnhold and S. Bleichroeder, Inc.	Arnhold & S. Bleichroeder, Inc.	Arnold and S. Bleichroeder, Inc.	5.____

TEST 11

DIRECTIONS: Answer the questions below on the basis of the following instructions: For each such numbered set of names, addresses, and numbers listed in Columns I and II, select your answer from the following options:
  A. The names in Columns I and II are different
  B. The addresses in Columns I and II are different
  C. The numbers in Columns I and II are different
  D. The names, addresses and numbers are identical

1. Francis Jones
   62 Stately Avenue
   96-12446

   Francis Jones
   62 Stately Avenue
   96-21446

   1.____

2. Julio Montez
   19 Ponderosa Road
   56-73161

   Julio Montez
   19 Ponderosa Road
   56-71361

   2.____

3. Mary Mitchell
   2314 Melbourne Drive
   68-92172

   Mary Mitchell
   2314 Melbourne Drive
   68-92172

   3.____

4. Harry Patterson
   25 Dunne Street
   14-33430

   Harry Patterson
   25 Dunne Street
   14-34330

   4.____

5. Patrick Murphy
   171 West Hosmer Street
   93-81214

   Patrick Murphy
   171 West Hosmer Street
   93-18214

   5.____

TEST 12

1. August Schultz
   816 St. Clair Avenue
   53-40149

   August Schultz
   816 St. Claire Avenue
   53-40149

   1.____

2. George Taft
   72 Runnymede Street
   47-04033

   George Taft
   72 Runnymede Street
   47-04023

   2.____

3. Angus Henderson
   1418 Madison Street
   81-76375

   Angus Henderson
   1418 Madison Street
   81-76375

   3.____

4. Carolyn Mazur
   12 Rivenlew Road
   38-99615

   Carolyn Mazur
   12 Rivervane Road
   38-99615

   4.____

5. Adele Russell
   1725 Lansing Lane
   72-91962

   Adela Russell
   1725 Lansing Lane
   72-91962

   5.____

TEST 13

DIRECTIONS: The following questions are based on the instructions given below. In each of the following questions, the 3-line name and address in Column I is the master-list entry, and the 3-line entry in Column II is the information to be checked against the master list.
If there is one line that is NOT exactly alike, mark your answer A.
If there are two lines NOT exactly alike, mark your answer B.
If there are three lines NOT exactly alike, mark your answer C.
If the lines ALL are exactly alike, mark your answer D.

1. Jerome A. Jackson
   1243 14th Avenue
   New York, N.Y. 10023

   Jerome A. Johnson
   1234 14th Avenue
   New York, N.Y. 10023

   1.____

2. Sophie Strachtheim
   33-28 Connecticut Ave.
   Far Rockaway, N.Y. 11697

   Sophie Strachtheim
   33-28 Connecticut Ave.
   Far Rockaway, N.Y. 11697

   2.____

3. Elisabeth NT. Gorrell
   256 Exchange St
   New York, N.Y. 10013

   Elizabeth NT. Correll
   256 Exchange St.
   New York, N.Y. 10013

   3.____

4. Maria J. Gonzalez
   7516 E. Sheepshead Rd.
   Brooklyn, N.Y. 11240

   Maria J. Gonzalez
   7516 N. Shepshead Rd.
   Brooklyn, N.Y. 11240

   4.____

5. Leslie B. Brautenweiler
   21-57A Seller Terr.
   Flushing, N.Y. 11367

   Leslie B. Brautenwieler
   21-75ASeiler Terr.
   Flushing, N.J. 11367

   5.____

KEY (CORRECT ANSWERS)

TEST 1	TEST 2	TEST 3	TEST 4	TEST 5	TEST 6	TEST 7
1. E	1. A	1. A	1. E	1. D	1. D	1. B
2. B	2. E	2. A	2. B	2. C	2. B	2. E
3. D	3. E	3. B	3. E	3. E	3. C	3. D
4. A	4. D	4. E	4. E	4. D	4. A	4. A
5. C	5. C	5. A	5. C	5. B	5. E	5. E

TEST 8	TEST 9	TEST 10	TEST 11	TEST 12	TEST 13
1. E	1. A	1. E	1. C	1. B	1. B
2. D	2. D	2. B	2. C	2. C	2. D
3. E	3. E	3. E	3. D	3. D	3. A
4. E	4. E	4. C	4. C	4. B	4. A
5. B	5. E	5. E	5. C	5. A	5. C

STENOGRAPHER-TYPIST EXAMINATION
CONTENTS

	Page
THE TYPING TEST	1
How the Test is Given	1
How the Test is Rated	1
How to Construct Additional Tests	2
Exhibit No. 6 Copying From Plain Paper	3
Practice Exercise	3
Test Exercise	4
Exhibit No. 7 Line Key for 5-Minute Typing Test	5
Speed	5
Accuracy	5
Exhibit No. 8 Maximum Number of Errors Permitted on 5-Minute Tests	6
THE DICTATION TEST	7
How the Transcript Booklet Works	7
How the Test is Administered	8
How the Answer Sheet is Scored	8
How to Construct Additional Tests	9
Exhibit No. 9 Dictation Test	11
Practice Dictation	11
Exhibit No. 10 Practice Dictation Transcript Sheet	13
Alphabetic World List	13
Transcript	13
Exhibit No. 11 Transcript Booklet-Dictation Test	15
Directions for Completing the Transcript	15
Directions for Marking the Separate Answer Sheet	15
Word List	16
Transcript	16
Exhibit No. 12 Key (Correct Answers)	18

THE TYPING TEST

In the test of ability to type, the applicant meets a single task, that of copying material exactly as it is presented. He must demonstrate how rapidly he can do so and with what accuracy. A specimen of the typing test is shown as Exhibit No. 6.

How The Test is Given

In order to follow usual examination procedure in giving the test, each competitor will need a copy of the test and two sheets of typewriter paper. About 15 minutes will be needed for the complete typing test.

Three minutes are allowed for reading the instructions on the face of the test and 3 minutes for the practice typing. The practice exercise consists of typing instructions as to spacing, capitalization, etc., and contains a warning that any erasures will be penalized. The practice typing helps make sure that the typewriter is functioning properly.

After the 3 minutes' practice typing, instruct the competitors to put fresh paper in their machines, and to turn the test page over and read the test for 2 minutes. After the 2 minutes, they are instructed to start typing the test. Five minutes are allowed for the test proper.

How the Test is Rated

The exercise must have been typed about once to meet the speed requirement of 40 words a minute. If this speed is not attained, the test is not scored for accuracy. As shown in Exhibit No. 7, a test paper that contains 17 lines meets the minimum speed requirement. Applicants have been instructed to begin and end each line precisely as in the printed test copy. From Exhibit No. 7 it can be quickly determined whether a typing test is to be rated for accuracy and, if so, the greatest number of errors permitted for the lines typed.

The next step is to compare the test paper with the printed test exercise and to mark and charge errors. The basic principles in charging typing errors are as follows:

Charge 1 for each—
WORD or PUNCTUATION MARK incorrectly typed or in which there is an erasure. (An error in spacing which follows an incorrect word or punctuation mark is not further charged.)
SERIES of consecutive words omitted, repeated, inserted, transposed, or erased. Charge for errors within such series, but the total charge cannot exceed the number of words.
LINE or part of line typed over other material, typed with all capitals, or apparently typed with the fingers on the wrong keys.
Change from the MARGIN where most lines are begun by the applicant or from the PARAGRAPAH INDENTION most frequently used by the applicant.

The typing score used in the official examination reflects both speed and accuracy, with accuracy weighted twice as heavily as speed. Other methods of rating typing often used in schools are based on gross words per minute or net words per minute (usually with not more than a fixed number of errors). Exhibit No. 8 will enable teachers and applicants to calculate typing proficiency in terms of gross words per minute and errors, and to determine whether that proficiency meets the minimum standards of eligibility required in the regular Civil Service examination.

Exhibit No. 8 gives the maximum number of errors permitted at various speeds for three different levels of typing ability. For example, at the minimum acceptable speed of 17 lines, or 40 gross words per minute, 3 errors are permitted for eligibility as GS-2 Clerk Typist or GS-3 Clerk-Stenographer. For GS-3 Clerk-Typist and GS-4 Clerk-Stenographer, and for GS-4 Clerk-Typist and GS-5 Clerk-Stenographer, higher standards of accuracy in relation to speed are reqired.

How to Construct Additional Tests

Here are some of the principal points followed by the examining staff in constructing typing tests so that the various tests will be comparable.

A passage should be subject matter that might reasonably be given a new typist in a government office. All words must be in sufficiently common use to be understood by most high school seniors, and the more difficult words must be dispersed throughout the passage rather than concentrated in one or two sentences. Sentence structure is not complicated. The length of the test exercise in Exhibit No. 6 is typical—21 lines of about 60 strokes each, with a total of about 1,250 strokes.

EXHIBIT NO. 6: COPYING FROM PLAIN COPY
(Part of the Stenographer-Typist Examination)

Read these directions carefully.

A practice exercise appears at the bottom of this sheet, and the test exercise itself is on the following page. First study these directions. Then, when the signal is given, begin to practice by typing the practice exercise below on the paper that has been given you. The examiner will tell you when to stop typing the practice exercise.

In both the practice and the test exercises, *space, paragraph, spell, punctuate, capitalize,* and *begin and end each line* precisely as shown in the exercises.

The examiner will tell you the exact time you will have to make repeated copies of the test exercise. Each time you complete the exercise, simply double space and begin again. If you fill up one side of the paper, turn it over and continue typing on the other side. Keep on typing until told to stop.

Keep in mind that you must meet minimum standards in both speed and accuracy and that, above these standards, accuracy is twice as important as speed. Make no erasures, insertions, or other corrections in this plain-copy test. Since errors are penalized whether or not they are erased or otherwise "corrected," it is best to keep on typing even though you detect an error.

PRACTICE EXERCISE

This practice exercise is similar in form and in difficulty to the one that you will be required to typewriter for the plain-copy test. You are to space, capitalize, punctuate, spell, and begin and end each line precisely as in the copy. Make no erasures, insertions, or other changes in this test because errors will be penalized even if they are erased or otherwise corrected. Practice typewriting this material on scratch paper until the examiner tells you to stop, remembering that for this examination it is more important for you to typewrite accurately than to typewrite rapidly.

TEST EXERCISE

    Because they have often learned to know types of architecture by decoration, casual observers sometimes fail to realize that the significant part of a structure is not the ornamentation but the body itself. Architecture, because of its close contact with human lives, is peculiarly and intimately governed by climate. For instance, a home built for comfort in the cold and snow of the northern areas of this country would be unbearably warm in a country with weather such as that of Cuba. A Cuban house, with its open court, would prove impossible to heat in a northern winter.

    Since the purpose of architecture is the construction of shelters in which human beings may carry on their numerous activities, the designer must consider not only climatic conditions but also the function of a building. Thus, although the climate of a certain locality requires that an auditorium and a hospital have several features in common, the purposes for which they will be used demand some difference in structure. For centuries builders have first complied with these two requirements and later added whatever ornamentation they wished. Logically, we should see as mere additions, not as basic parts, the details by which we identify architecture.

EACH TIME YOU REACH THIS POINT, DOUBLE SPACE AND BEGIN AGAIN.

EXHIBIT NO. 7: LINE KEY FOR 5-MINUTE TYPING TEST SHOWING MAXIMUM NUMBER OF ERRORS PERMISSIBLE FOR VARIOUS TYPING SPEEDS, AT GRADES GS-2 TYPIST AND GS-3 STENOGRAPHER

SPEED: In the following example, more than 16 lines have been typed for any speed rating. This sample key is constructed on the premise that if the competitor made the first stroke in her final line (even if it was an error), she is given credit for that line in determining the gross words per minute.

ACCURACY: The gross words per minute typed, at any line is the number *outside* the parentheses opposite that line. The numbers *in* the parentheses show the maximum number of errors permitted for that number of gross words per minute typed. The number of errors permitted increases with the speed. (This sample key shows the requirements for GS-2 Typist and GS-3 Stenographer. Exhibit No. 8 shows the standards for higher grades.) If the number of strokes per line were different, this table would have to be altered accordingly.

	Maximum Number of Errors Per Gross Words Per Minute Typed	
	1st Typing of Exercise	2nd Typing of Exercise
Because they have often learned to know types of architec		52(7)
tecture by decoration, casual observers sometimes fail to		54(7)
realize that the significant part of a structure is not the		56(8)
ornamentation but the body itself. Architecture, because		59(8)
of its close contact with human lives, is peculiarly and		61(9)
intimately governed by climate. For instance, a home built		64(9)
for comfort in the cold and snow of the northern areas of		66(10)
this country would be unbearably warm in a country with		68(10)
weather such as that of Cuba. A Cuban house, with its open		71(11)
court, would prove impossible to heat in a northern winter.		73(11)
Since the purpose of architecture is the construction of		76(12)
shelters in which human beings may carry on their numerous		78(12)
activities, the designer must consider not only climatic con-		80(12)[2]
ditions, but also the function of a building. Thus, although		
the climate of a certain locality requires that an auditorium		
and a hospital have several features in common, the purposes		
for which they will be used demand some difference in struc-	40(3)[1]	
ture. For centuries builders have first complied with these	42(4)	
two requirements and later added whatever ornamentation they	44(5)	
wished. Logically, we should see as mere additions, not as	47(6)	
basic parts, the details by which we identify architecture.	49(6)	

[1] The minimum rated speed is 40 gross words per minute for typing from printed copy.

[2] Any material typed after 80 gross words per minute (which is considered 100 in speed) is *not* rated for accuracy.

Note: The number of errors shown above must be proportionately increased for tests which are longer than 5 minutes.

EXHIBIT NO. 8: MAXIMUM NUMBER OF ERRORS PERMITTED ON 5-MINUTE TESTS AT VARIOUS SPEEDS FOR TYPING SCORES REQUIRED FOR TYPIST AND STENOGRAPHER POSITIONS

SPEED	MAXIMUM NUMBER OF ERRORS PERMITTED		
Gross Words Per Minute	GS-2 Clerk-Typist GS-3 Clerk-Stenographer	GS-3 Clerk-Typist GS-4 Clerk-Stenographer	GS-4 Clerk-Typist GS-5 Clerk-Stenographer
Under 40	Ineligible	Ineligible	Ineligible
40	3	9	2
41-42	4	4	2
43-44	5	4	2
45-47	6	5	3
48-49	6	5	3
50-52	7	6	4
53-54	7	6	4
55-56	8	7	5
57-59	8	7	5
60-61	9	8	6
62-64	9	8	7
65-66	10	9	7
67-68	10	9	8
69-71	11	10	8
72-73	11	10	9
74-76	12	11	10
77-78	12	11	10
79-80	12	12	10

NOTE: The number of errors shown above must be proportionately increased for tests which are longer than 5 minutes.

THE DICTATION TEST

The dictation test includes a practice dictation and a test exercise, each consisting of 240 words. The rate of dictation is 80 words a minute.

The dictation passages are nontechnical subject matter that might be given a stenographer in a government office. Sentence structure is not complicated and sentences are not extremely long or short. The words average 1.5 syllables in length.

As shown in Exhibit No. 9, each dictation passage is printed with spacing to show the point that the dictator should reach at the end of each 10 seconds in order to maintain an even dictation rate of 80 words a minute. This indication of timing is one device for assisting all examiners to conform to the intended dictation rate. All examiners are also sent instructions for dictating and a sample passage to be used in practicing dictating before the day of the test. By using these devices for securing uniform dictating and by providing alternate dictation passages that are as nearly equal as possible, the Commission can give each applicant a test that is neither harder nor easier than those given others competing for the same jobs.

The test differs from the conventional dictation test in the method of transcribing the notes. The applicant is not required to type a transcript of the notes, but follows a procedure that permits machine scoring of the test. When typewritten transcripts were still required, examiners rated the test by comparing every word of a competitor's paper with the material dictated and charging errors. Fairness to those competing for employment required that comparable errors be penalized equally. Because of the variety of errors and combinations of error that can be made in transcripts, the scoring of typewritten transcripts required considerable training and consumed much time—many months for large nationwide examination. After years of experimentation, a transcript booklet procedure was devised that simplified and speeded the scoring procedure.

Today, rating is decentralized to U.S. Civil Service Commission area offices, and test scores can be furnished quickly and accurately. The transcript booklet makes these improvements possible.

How the Transcript Booklet Works

The transcript booklet (see Exhibit No. 11) gives the stenographer parts of the dictated passage, but leaves blank spaces where many of the words belong. With adequate shorthand notes, the stenographer can readily fit the correct words into the blank spaces, which are numbered 1 through 125. At the left of the printed partial transcript is a list of words, each word with a capital letter A, B, C, or D beside it. Knowing from the notes what word belongs in a blank space, the competitor looks for it among the words in the list. The letter beside the word or phrase in the list is the answer to be marked in the space on the transcript. In the list there are other words that a competitor with inadequate notes might guess belong in that space, but the capital letter beside these words would be an incorrect answer. (Some persons find it helpful to write the word or the shorthand symbol in the blank space before looking for it in the word list. There is no objection to doing this.)

Look, for example, at the Practice Dictation Transcript Sheet, Exhibit No. 10, question 10. The word dictated is "physical"; it is in the word list with a capital "D." In the transcript, blank number 10 should be answered "D."

None of the words in the list is marked "E." This is because the answer "E" is reserved for any question when the word dictated for that spot does not appear in the list. Every transcript booklet has spots for which the list does not include the correct words. This provision reduces the possibility that competitors may guess correct answers.

After the stenographer has written the letter of the missing word or phrase in each numbered blank of the transcript, he transfers the answers to the proper spaces on the answer sheet. Directions for marking the separate answer sheet are given on page 1 of Exhibit No. 11.

This transcription procedure should not cause any good stenographer to make a poor showing on the examination. To this end, illustrations of the procedure are included in a sheet of samples that is mailed to each applicant with the notice of when and where to report for examination. Again in the examination room, the applicant uses such a transcript on the practice dictation before the actual dictation is given. A major objective in preparing this publication is to further insure that each prospective competitor is made to feel at ease about using this method of handling how good the notes are.

Use of the transcript booklet and transfer of answers to the answer sheet are clerical tasks that are not part of transcribing by typewriter. Most stenographic positions involve clerical duties for some percentage of the time and it is reasonable, therefore, to include clerical tasks in the examination. Although some unsuccessful competitors for stenographic positions attribute their failure to the use of transcript booklets, analysis of many test papers, notes, and transcripts has shown the frequency of clerical error in this test to be negligible.

How the Test is Administered

Each competitor will need a copy of the Practice Dictation Transcript Sheet (Exhibit No. 10), a copy of the Transcript Booklet (Exhibit No. 11), and an answer sheet (Exhibit No. 2). These should be distributed at the times indicated below.

The Practice Dictation of Exhibit No. 9 should be dictated at the rate indicated by the 10 second divisions in which it is printed. This will be at the rate of 80 words a minute. Then each competitor should be given a copy of the Practice Dictation Transcript Sheet and allowed 7 minutes to study the instructions and to transcribe part of the practice dictation.

The text exercise (reverse of Exhibit No. 9) should also be dictated at the rate of 80 words a minute, for 3 minutes. Each competitor should be given a Transcript Booklet and an answer sheet. He should be told that he will have 3 minutes for reading the directions on the face page, followed by 30 minutes for writing answers in the blank spaces, and then 10 minutes for transferring his answers to the answer sheet. These time limits are those used in the official examination and have been found ample.

How the Answer Sheet is Scored

The correct answers for the test are given in Exhibit No. 12. A scoring stencil may be prepared by copying these answers on a blank answer sheet and then punching out the marked answer boxes. Directions for using the scoring stencil are given at the top of Exhibit No. 12.

In some rare instances where the typewritten transcript is still used, the passing standard on the total transcript is 24 or fewer errors for GS-3 Clerk-Stenographer, and 12 or fewer errors for GS-4. Comparable standards on the parts of the dictation measured by the machine-scored method of transcription are 14 or fewer errors for GS-3, and 6 or fewer errors for GS-4 positions.

A stenographer who can take dictation at 80 words a minute with this degree of accuracy is considered fully qualified. Positions such as Reporting Stenographer and Shorthand Reporter require ability to take dictation at much higher speeds. The test for Reporting Stenographer is dictated at 120 words a minute. Two rates of dictation, 160 and 175 words a minute, are used for the Shorthand Reporter tests for different grade levels.

How to Construct Additional Tests

A teacher who has examined students by the tests in this part may wish to re-examine some of them after a period of further training. For this purpose, it is desirable to use new tests rather than to repeat the same test too often. If additional test material is needed, it should be constructed in accordance with the following principles in order to keep alternative tests comparable.

As already indicated, the subject matter and the vocabulary should not be technical or too unusual; they should appear to be part of the day-to-day business of an efficient government office. In view of the broad range of activities of Federal agencies, this restriction still allows a wide range of subject matter.

For 3 minutes of dictation at 80 words a minute, the exercise should contain 240 words. The average number of syllables should be about 1.5. Sentences should be straightforward, rather than of complicated grammatical construction. At the same time, they should not be short and choppy.

Before the transcript booklet is made, a skeleton transcript should be prepared. One way of beginning is to choose words and groups of words that should be tested. A total of about 140 words of the complete dictation passage should be chosen for testing, since some of the 125 numbered blank spaces in the transcript booklet should represent more than one word. As shown in the transcripts in Exhibits No. 10 and 11, the words selected for testing are not chosen simply by taking every other word; rather, they are single words or series of words distributed throughout the dictation passage. The first word of any sentence should not be used as a test word.

The dictation passage should be divided into four sections of about equal length with a section always breaking at the end of a sentence. A worksheet similar to that shown below should be prepared for each section.

For illustration of the next steps, look at the reverse side of the Practice Dictation Transcript Sheet, Exhibit No. 10; let the two sentences at the bottom of that page represent the dictation. The words that have been chosen for testing are "bring," "about," "to visit," "their," and so on; these words or phrases have been numbered 16, 17, etc. For a convenient worksheet, ruled paper can be divided into columns headed A, B, C, D, and E. Now the words chosen for the blanks should be distributed at random in the various columns. At this point the worksheet for this part of the test will look like the following:

	A	B	C	D	E
16	bring				
17					about
18		to visit			
19				their	
20				to discuss	
21					treatment
22			correction		
23					value
24		see			
25	is not				

(and so on)

Next, think of several plausible errors for each of the blanks; that is, a word beginning with the same sound, a word that fits the preceding or the following word almost as a cliché, etc. Avoid any error that is too conspicuously wrong or too clearly a misfit with printed auxiliaries or articles to present any difficulty. Place each plausible error in column A, B, C, or D of the worksheet, *avoiding* the column that contains the *answer*. The worksheet will now look like the columns below.

Experience will bring out situations that must be avoided, such as use of the same word in more than one column.

Each word in columns A, B, C, and D takes the letter at the head of the column. The words in these columns are grouped in alphabetic order to become the "Word List" for the section of the transcript covered by this worksheet. Since instructions provide that E is to be selected when the exact answer is not listed, the words in column E are NOT included in the "Word List." The sentences are presented with numbered blanks as the "Transcript."

	A	B	C	D	E
16	bring	promote	discuss	understand	
17	all				about
18	visit	to visit	at	during	
19	(all)		young	their	
20	to discover	undertake	{to endorse {indicated	to discuss	
21	treatments				treatment
22	reducing	collection	correction	recognizing	
23	friend	volume		virtue	value
24	know	see	say	satisfied	
25	is not	is	soon	{knows {insisted	

(and so on)

EXHIBIT NO. 9: DICTATION TEST
(Part of the Stenographer-Typist Examination)

PRACTICE DICTATION

INSTRUCTIONS TO THE EXAMINER: This Practice Dictation and one exercise will be dictated at the rate of 80 words a minute. Do not dictate the punctuation except for periods, but dictate with the expression that the punctuation indicates. Use a watch with a second hand to enable you to read the exercises at the proper speed.

Exactly on a minute, start dictating.

	Finish reading each two lines at the number of seconds indicated below.
I realize that this practice dictation is not a part of the examination	10
proper and is not to be scored. (Period) The work of preventing and correcting	20
physical defects in children is becoming more effective as a result of a change	30
in the attitude of many parents. (Period) In order to bring about this change	40
mothers have been invited to visit the schools when their children are being examined	50
and to discuss the treatment necessary for the correction of defects. (Period)	1 min.
There is a distinct value in having a mother see that her child is not the	10
only one who needs attention. (Period) Otherwise a few parents might feel that they	20
were being criticized by having the defects of their children singled out for medical	30
treatment. (Period) The special classes that have been set up have shown the value of	40
the scientific knowledge that has been applied in the treatment of children. (Period)	50
In these classes the children have been taught to exercise by a trained teacher	2 min.
under medical supervision. (Period) The hours of the school day have been divided	10
between school work and physical activity that helps not only to correct their defects	20
but also to improve their general physical condition. (Period) This method of treatment	30
has been found to be very effective except for those who have severe medical	40
defects. (Period) Most parents now see how desirable it is to have these classes	50
that have been set up in the regular school system to meet special needs. (Period)	3 min.

After dictating the practice, pause for 15 seconds to permit competitors to complete their notes. Then continue in accordance with the directions for conducting the examination.

After the Practice Dictation Transcript has been completed, dictate the test from the following.

Exactly on a minute, start dictating.

	Finish reading each two lines at the number of seconds indicated below.
The number enrolled in shorthand classes in the high schools has shown a marked increase. (Period)	10
Today this subject is one of the most popular offered in the field of	20
business education. (Period) When shorthand was first taught, educators claimed that it was of	30
value mainly in sharpening the powers of observation and discrimination. (Period)	40
However, with the growth of business and the increased demand for office workers,	50
educators have come to realize the importance of stenography as a vocational	1 min.
tool. (Period) With the differences in the aims of instruction came changes in	10
the grade placement of the subject. (Period) The prevailing thought has always been that it	20
should be offered in high school. (Period) When the junior high school first came into	30
being, shorthand was moved down to that level with little change in the manner in which	40
the subject was taught. (Period) It was soon realized that shorthand had no place there	50
because the training had lost its vocational utility by the time the student could	2 min.
graduate. (Period) Moreover, surveys of those with education only through junior	10
high school seldom found them at work as stenographers. (Period) For this reason, shorthand	20
was returned to the high school level and is offered as near as possible to the time	30
of graduation so that the skill will be retained when the student takes a job. (Period)	40
Because the age at which students enter office jobs has advanced, there is now	50
a tendency to upgrade business education into the junior college. (Period)	3 min.

After completing the dictation, pause of 15 seconds.
Give a Transcript to each competitor.

EXHIBIT NO. 10: PRACTICE DICTATION TRANSCRIPT SHEET
(Part of the Stenographer-Typist Examination)

The transcript below is part of the material that was dictated to you for practice, except that many of the words have been left out. From your notes, you are to tell what the missing words are. Proceed as follows:

Compare your notes with the transcript and, when you come to a blank in the transcript, decide what word or words belong there. For example, you will find that the word "practice" belongs in blank number 1. Look at the Word List to see whether you can find the same word there. Notice what letter (A, B, C, or D) is printed beside it, and write that letter in the blank. For example, the word "practice" is listed, followed by the letter "B." We have already written "B" in blank number 1 to show you how you are to record your choice. Now decide what belongs in each of the other blanks. (You may also write the word or words, or the shorthand for them, if you wish.) The same word may belong in more than one blank. If the exact answer is not listed, write "E" in the blank.

TRANSCRIPT

I realize that this __B__ dictation is ____
                         1   2

a ____ of the ____ ____ and is ____ ____
   3   4   5   6   7

scored.
    The work of ____ and ____ ____ defects in
                        8   9   10

____ is becoming more ____ as a ____ a
 11   12   13

change in the ____ of many ____ ....
                14   15

ALPHABETIC WORD LIST	
about-B	paper-B
against-C	parents-B
attitude-A	part-C
being-D	physical-D
childhood-B	portion-D
children-A	practical-A
correcting-C	practice-B
doctors-B	preliminary-D
effective-D	preventing-B
efficient-A	procedure-A
examination-A	proper-C
examining-C	reason for-A
for-B	result-B
health-B	result of-C
mothers-C	schools-C
never-C	to be-C
not-D	to prevent-A

Each numbered blank in the Transcript is a question. You will be given a separate answer sheet like the sample here, to which you will transfer your answers. The answer sheet has a numbered row of boxes for each question. The answer for blank number 1 is "B." We have already transferred this to number 1 in the Sample Answer Sheet, by darkening the box under "B."

Now transfer your answer for each of questions 2 through 15 to the answer sheet. That is, beside each number on the answer sheet find the letter that is the same as the letter you wrote in the blank with the same number in the transcript, and darken the box below that letter.

After you have marked 15, continue with blank number 16 on the next page WITHOUT WAITING FOR A SIGNAL.

TRANSCRIPT (continued)

In order to ____ ____ this change, mothers
           16   17
have been invited ____ the schools when ____
                 18   19
children are being examined and ____ the ____
                              20   21
necessary for the ____ of defects. There is a
                  22
distinct ____ in having a mother ____ that her
       23   24
child ____ the only one who needs attention....
       25

ALPHABETIC WORD LIST	
all-A	reducing-A
at-C	satisfied-D
bring-A	say-C
collection-B	see-B
correction-C	soon-C
discuss-C	their-D
during-D	to discover-A
friend-A	to discuss-D
indicated-C	to endorse-C
insisted-D	to visit-B
is-B	treatments-A
is not-A	understand-D
know-A	undertake-B
knows-D	virtue-D
needed-B	visit-A
promote-B	volume-B
recognizing-D	young-C

Your notes should show that the word "bring" goes in blank 16, and "about" in blank 17. But "about" is *not in the list*; so "E" should be your answer for Question 17.

The two words, "to visit-B," are needed for 18, and the one word "visit-A," would be an incorrect answer.

Fold this page so that the Correct Answers to Samples 1 through 8, below, will lie beside the Sample Answer Sheet you marked for those questions. Compare your answers with the correct answers. Then fold the page and compare the correct answers with your answers for 9 through 15. If one of your answers does not agree with the correct answer, again compare your notes with the samples and make certain you understand the instructions. The correct answers for 16 through 25 are as follows: 16-A, 17-E, 18-B, 19-D, 20-D, 21-E, 22-C, 23-E, 24-B, and 25-A.

For the actual test, you will use a separate answer sheet. As scoring will be done by an electronic scoring machine, it is important that you follow directions carefully. Use a medium No. 2 pencil. You must keep your mark for a question within the box. If you have to erase a mark, be sure to erase it completely. Mark only one answer for each question.

For any stenographer who missed the practice dictation, part of it is given below:

"I realize that this practice dictation is not a part of the examination proper and is not to be scored.

"The work of preventing and correcting physical defects in children is becoming more effective as a result of a change in the attitude of many parents. In order to bring about this change, mothers have been invited to visit the schools when their children are being examined and to discuss the treatment necessary for the correction of defects. There is a distinct value in having a mother see that her child is not the only one who needs attention..."

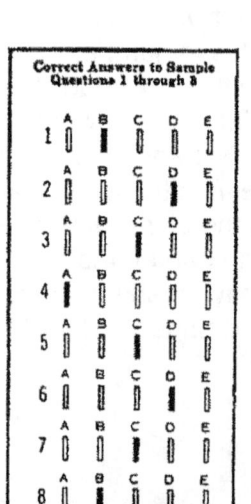

186

EXHIBIT NO. 11: TRANSCRIPT BOOKLET – DICTATION TEST
(Part of Stenographer-Typist Examination)

Directions for Completing the Transcript

  A transcript of the dictation you have just taken is given on Pages 15 and 16. As in the transcript for the practice dictation, there are numbered blank spaces for many of the words that were dictated. You are to compare your notes with the transcript and, when you come to a blank, decide what word or words belong there. For most of the blanks the words are included in the list beside the transcript; each is followed by a letter, A, B, C, or D. To show that you know which word or words belong in each blank space, you are to write the letter in the blank. You are to write E if the exact answer is NOT listed. (In addition, you may write the word or words, or the shorthand for them, if you wish.) The same choice may belong in more than one blank.
  After you have compared your notes with the transcript and have chosen the answer for each blank space, you will be given additional time to transfer your answers to a separate answer sheet.

Directions for Marking the Separate Answer Sheet

  On the answer sheet, each question number stands for the blank with the same number in the transcript. For each number, you are to darken the box below the letter that is the same as the letter you wrote in the transcript. (The answers in this booklet will not be rated.) Be sure to use your pencil and record your answers on the separate answer sheet. You must keep your mark within the bod. If you have to erase a mark, be sure to erase it completely. Make only one mark for each question.
  Work quickly so that you will be able to finish in the time allowed. First, you should darken the boxes on the answer sheet for the blanks you have lettered. You may continue to use your notes if you have not finished writing letters in the blanks in the transcript, or if you wish to make sure you have lettered them correctly.

TRANSCRIPT

The number ____ in shorthand ____ ____
        1   2   3
high schools has ____ a ____ ____. Today ____
                   4   5   6   7
____ is one of the most ____ ____ ____ ____ of
 8   9   10   11   12
business ____. When ____ ____ ____ ____
          13   14   15   16   17
educators ____ that it ____ ____ ____ in ____
            18   19   20   21   22
____ ____ of ____ and ____.
 23   24   25   26

...However, ____ the growth of ____ and the ____
              27   28   29
for ____ ____, ____ have ____ ____ the ____
     30   31   32   33   34   35
of ____ ____ ____ ____ in the ____ ____ of the
   36   37   38   39   40   41
____. The ____ ____ ____ ____ that ____
 42   43   44   45   46   47
____ ____ in ____.
 48   49   50

ALPHABETIC WORD LIST	
Write E if the answer is NOT listed	
administration-C	observation-B
along the-B	observing-A
area-A	offered-C
at first-A	of value-C
claimed-C	open-A
classes-B	popular-B
concluded-D	power-B
could be-D	powers-D
courses-C	practical-A
decrease-D	shaping-A
discriminating-C	sharpen-B
discrimination-D	shorthand-D
education-B	shown-C
enrolled-D	stenography-B
entering-A	study-C
field-D	subject-A
first-D	taught-D
given-B	that-C
great-C	the-D
increase-A	these-B
in the-D	this-A
known-D	thought-B
line-C	to be-A
mainly-B	training-D
marked-B	valuable-A
mostly-D	vast-A

ALPHABETIC WORD LIST	
Write E if the answer is NOT listed	
a change-D	offered-C
administration-C	office-A
aims-A	official-C
always been-A	often been-B
begun-D	ought to be-B
businesses-A	place-B
came-D	placement-D
changes-B	prevailing-B
come-C	rule-D
defects-B	schools-D
demand-B	shorthand-D
demands-A	should be-A
differences-D	significance-C
education-B	stenography-B
educators-D	study-A
for-D	subject-A
given-B	thinking-C
grade-C	this-A
grading-B	thought-B
has-C	tool-B
had-B	to realize-B
have come-A	to recognize-B
high school-B	valuable-A
increased-D	vocational-C
increasing-C	when the-D
institutions-D	with-A
instruction-C	without-C
it-B	workers-C

…When the ___ school ___ ___ ___, ___
           57   58 59 60   61
was ___ to ___ ___ with ___ ___ in ___
    62   63   64   65   66   67
___ ___ the ___ was ___. It was ___
68 69   70   71   72
___ that ___ ___ place ___ ___ the ___
73   74 75   76   77   78
had ___ ___ ___ ___ by the ___ the
    79   80 81 82   83
___ ___ ___.
84   85   86

ALPHABETIC WORD LIST	
Write E if the answer is NOT listed	
became-B	moved-C
because-B	moved down-B
came-D	occupational-B
change-A	recognized-A
changed-C	shorthand-D
could-C	since-C
could be-D	soon-C
date-D	stenography-B
first-D	student-A
graduate-D	students-C
graduated-B	study-C
had little-C	subject-A
had no-A	taught-D
here-D	that-C
high-C	the-D
into being-A	their-B
into business-C	there-B
junior high-D	this-A
less-B	time-B
lessened-C	training-D
level-C	usefulness-B
little-A	utility-C
lost-D	vocational-C
manner-B	which-A
method-C	

…Moreover, ___ of ___ with ___ ___ ___
            87   88   89 90 91
___ school ___ ___ them ___ as ___. For
92   93 94   95   96
___ ___, shorthand was ___ to the ___ ___ ___
97 98   99   100 101
and is ___ as ___ ___ to the ___ ___ ___
      102   103 104   105 106 107
___ the skill ___ ___ ___ ___ the student
108   109 110 111 112
___ a ___. Because the ___ ___ students
113 114   115 116
___ office ___ ___ ___, there is ___ a
117   118 119 120   121
___ to ___ ___ education ___ the junior
122   123 124   125
college.

ALPHABETIC WORD LIST	
Write E if the answer is NOT listed	
advanced-A	reason-B
age-A	reasons-D
as far as-C	retained-B
at which-D	school-A
at work-A	secretaries-D
be-B	secures-D
date-D	seldom-C
education-B	showed-A
enter-D	so-A
found-D	stenographers-C
graduating-A	studies-B
graduation-C	surveys-A
has-C	takes-A
high school-B	taught-D
in-A	tendency-B
in order-D	that-C
increased-D	there-B
into-B	this-A
job-B	through-D
junior high-D	time-B
level-C	training-D
may be-C	undertake-A
near as-A	until-A
nearly as-C	upgrade-D
offered-C	when-C
often-B	which-A
only-B	will-B
possible-D	would-D
rarely-D	working-B

KEY (CORRECT ANSWERS)

EXHIBIT NO. 12: SCORING STENCIL-RIGHT ANSWERS

If the competitor marked more than one answer to any question, draw a line through the answer boxes for the question. To make a stencil, punch out the answers on this page or on a separate answer sheet. Place this punched key over a competitor's sheet. Count the right answers. DO NOT GIVE CREDIT FOR DOUBLE ANSWERS.

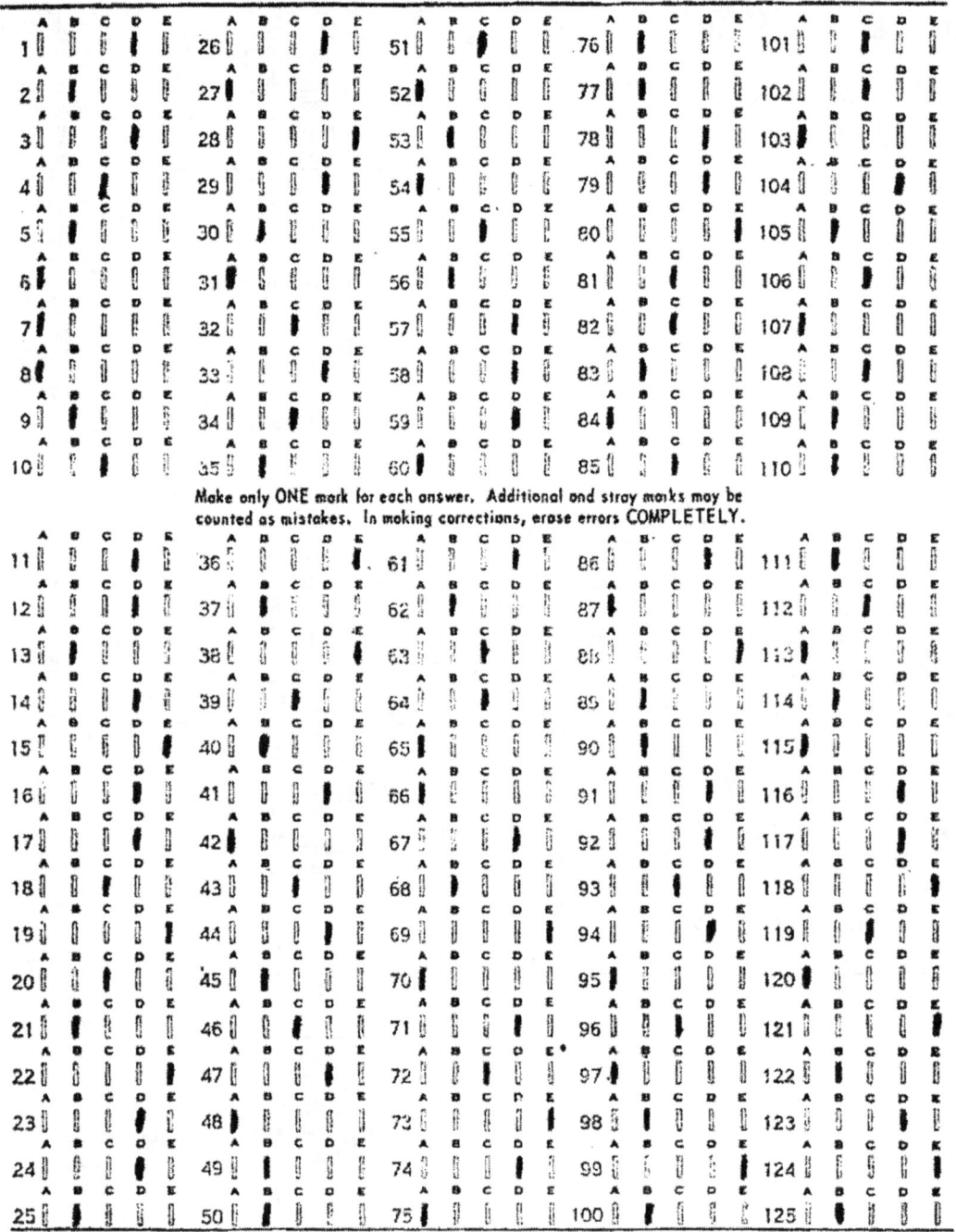

www.ingramcontent.com/pod-product-compliance
Lightning Source LLC
Chambersburg PA
CBHW080731230426
43665CB00020B/2704